VIRGINIA

A Pictorial History

VIRGINIA

PARKE ROUSE, Jr.

CHARLES SCRIBNER'S SONS

New York

For my brothers,
Randolph Dashiell Rouse, William Dashiell Rouse,
and the late John Dashiell Rouse, 1st Lieut., AUS

Title Page
St. George Tucker House, Williamsburg
Photo: Thomas L. Williams, Colonial Williamsburg

Page viii-ix
Map of Virginia, from Mitchell's *New General Atlas,* Philadelphia, 1880

Editor   NORMAN KOTKER

Editorial Assistant   PATRICIA LUCA

Art Director   RONALD FARBER

Contents

SOURCES AND ACKNOWLEDGMENTS *vi*

MAP OF VIRGINIA *viii*

INTRODUCTION *3*

A PICTORIAL HISTORY *19*

The Great Commonwealth *20*

The Revolution Begins *72*

An Age of Growth *86*

The Civil War *142*

Reconciliation *204*

A New Era *272*

BIBLIOGRAPHY *341*

PICTURE CREDITS *343*

INDEX *347*

Sources and Acknowledgments

The systematic collecting of prints and photographs is a relatively recent activity of American museums. For that reason, Virginia's pictorial record can be found in no single place in complete form; the best a compiler of a pictorial history can do is search the standard archives and try to fill gaps with pictures from private sources. In the case of a state as old as Virginia, this is a real challenge.

The recent growth of picture archives, however, has greatly eased the anthologist's task. A half-dozen institutions now have extensive collections dealing with the Old Dominion. Others afford specialized views, as in the Mariners Museum library at Newport News and in the Colonial Williamsburg Foundation's record of eighteenth-century life and crafts.

Much Virginia material is to be found in such repositories as the Library of Congress, which has the Mathew Brady photographs of the Civil War; and the New York Public Library, which has the Arents tobacco collection. Not until recently did any Virginia institution acquire comparable riches. Today, however, the Virginia State Library, the Virginia Historical Society library, and the Valentine Museum library are all actively collecting graphics once threatened by loss or dispersion. To a lesser degree, colleges and universities, public libraries, city governments, military bases, large corporations, and local museums are saving pictorial archives, and I have searched many of them.

Virginia's legacy of paintings, drawings, and prints from her first two centuries is not extensive. The first English immigrants were farmers who left little graphic record of themselves. As plantations grew, a few affluent planters and their wives were portrayed by English artists like Peter Lely, Godfrey Kneller, and Charles Bridges. Later came such itinerant portraitists as Gustavus Hesselius, John Durand, John Wollaston, and others whose names are unknown, followed by the revolutionary generation of the Peale family, Jonathan Trumbull, Benjamin West, and Gilbert Stuart.

Even folk artists were rare in colonial Virginia except in the Germanic counties of the uplands, if one is to judge from the Abby Aldrich Rockefeller Folk Art Collection in Williamsburg and other folk art archives. Virginia also had little early printing; not until 1730 did Williamsburg acquire an indigenous press, thereafter producing a thin stream of pamphlets and an occasional book, along with the weekly *Virginia Gazette.*

Artists and presses increased in the nineteenth century as Norfolk, Richmond, Petersburg, and Alexandria grew to provide patronage. Among artists who lived or painted in the state before the Civil War were Laurence and Thomas Sully, William James Hubard, John A. Elder, James Warrell, Edward F. Peticolas, James Ford, George Cooke, John Gadsby Chapman (his son Conrad painted during and after the war), and the prolific genre painter William Ludwell Sheppard. From them and from visiting artists like Winslow Homer and Alfred Waud, who accompanied federal troops in 1861–65, we inherit a rich graphic record of the war, much of it once published in *Harper's Weekly, Leslie's Illustrated Newspaper, Scribner's,* and *The Century.*

The Civil War also left a photographic record, filmed by such pioneers as Mathew Brady of New York, Michael Miley of Lexington, and George Cook—not to be confused with painter George Cooke—of South Carolina and Richmond. In four short years photography became the dominant pictorial medium of industrial America.

Several significant collections of early prints and portraits were made by Virginia collectors in the twentieth century, but it remained for Alexander Weddell, Richmond diplomat and antiquarian, to bring these pictorial archives into focus. An exhibition by the Virginia Historical Society in 1929 resulted in publication the next year of *Virginia Historical Portraiture, 1585–1930,* edited by Mr. Weddell. In 1931 the Richmond Public Library held an exhibition that resulted in 1932 in *Richmond Virginia in Old Prints, 1737–1887,* also edited by Mr. Weddell.

The pictorial archive of the State Library began its real growth during the tenure of Wilmer L. Hall as state librarian, from 1934 to 1946. This was accelerated by creation of the library's illustrated quarterly, *Virginia Cavalcade,* in 1951, under the editorship until 1958 of W. Edwin Hemphill. In charge of prints and photographs since 1956 has been Mrs. Katherine Smith, who has aided me far beyond duty's call.

The Valentine Museum's photographic collection began before the 1930s with its receipt of prints and negatives by Robert Lancaster, then secretary of the Virginia Historical Society; Palmer Gray, who photographed in Richmond, Norfolk, Alexandria, and Fredericksburg; Edythe Beveridge, a pioneer Virginia news photographer; Mary Wingfield Scott, a leading architectural historian of Richmond; and by George Cook and his son Huestis, Richmond photographers of the Civil War and Reconstruction. As librarian of the Valentine from 1930 to 1963, Mrs. Ralph Catterall added immeasurably to its usefulness. To her and her successors, Miss Elizabeth Dance and, currently, Mrs. Stuart Gibson, I express gratitude. In its collection of Richmond photographs, prints, playbills, and ephemera, the Valentine boasts a civic record hardly excelled in America.

The Virginia Historical Society, also headquartered in Richmond, has developed a worthy pictorial archive during the tenure of its present director, John Melville Jennings. To him and to Mrs. Kenneth Southall, curator of special collections, go my thanks.

I also express gratitude to the following:

Mrs. Robert Anderson, Valentine Museum; Mrs. Eugene Sheldon and Hugh DeSamper, Colonial Williamsburg Foundation; Mrs. Jacqueline Taylor, Jamestown Foundation; John Lochhead, Mariners Museum; Ross Weeks, Jr., College of William and Mary; Major Edwin L. Dooley, Virginia Military Institute; William H. Fishback, Jr., University of Virginia; Robert Keefe, Washington and Lee University.

John Mitchell, Syms-Eaton Museum, Hampton; James E. True, Southwest Virginia Museum, Big Stone Gap; David Clinger, Reynolds Metals Company, Richmond; Brick Ryder, City of Richmond; Miss Anne Newsome, Hampton Coliseum; Klaus Wust, Edinburg; Philip Flournoy and Marshall Garber, Virginia State Chamber of Commerce, Richmond; Fred Haseltine, Virginia Museum of Fine Arts, Richmond; Miss Mary Morris Watt, Richmond Newspapers, Inc.

Dr. Janet Kimbrough, Mrs. V. Lee Kirby, Drewry Jones, and John Henderson, Williamsburg; Robert B. Smith, Daily Press, Inc., Newport News; Mrs. Helen Duprey Bullock, Washington, D.C.; Robert A. Murdock and Mrs. John Sowder, Association for the Preservation of Virginia Antiquities, Richmond; James Haskett, Colonial National Historic Park, Yorktown; Albert W. Coates, Jr., Virginia Department of Highways, Richmond; Judge John Tisdale, Clarksville; George Myers, Danville Textile and Tobacco Museum, Danville.

Powell Glass, Jr., publisher, *Lynchburg News* and *Daily Advance,* Lynchburg; Thomas L. Williams, photographer, Williamsburg; William O'Donovan, *The Virginia Gazette,* Williamsburg; Mrs. Roberta Ingles Steele, Radford; Fred P. Painter, Woodstock; Ralph Bingham, New Market; John Curtis, the Bookpress, Williamsburg; Francis Berkeley, University of Virginia; Royster Lyle, George C. Marshall Library, Lexington.

Finally, I would like to express gratitude to several friends who kindly read portions of the manuscript. These include Alexander Crosby Brown, Newport News; Thad Tate, director of the Institute of Early American History and Culture, Williamsburg; Judge and Mrs. Ralph Catterall, Richmond; Dr. Chester Bradley, former director, The Casemate Museum, Old Point Comfort; Mrs. John Minor, Williamsburg; and my wife, Betsy Gayle Rouse, whose patience and helpfulness know no end.

PARKE ROUSE, JR.

Williamsburg, Virginia

Virginia—1880

An 1880 map shows the vast area covered by Virginia before the Civil War. By the time this map was printed, West Virginia had broken away from the commonwealth. An extensive network of railroads reached into every part of Virginia, connecting Richmond with all the other major cities.

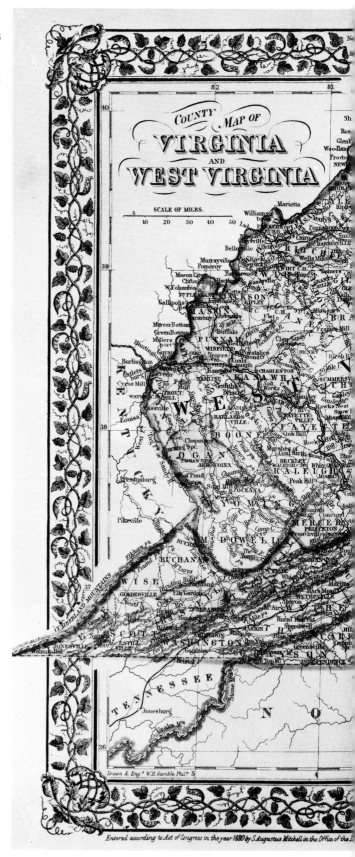

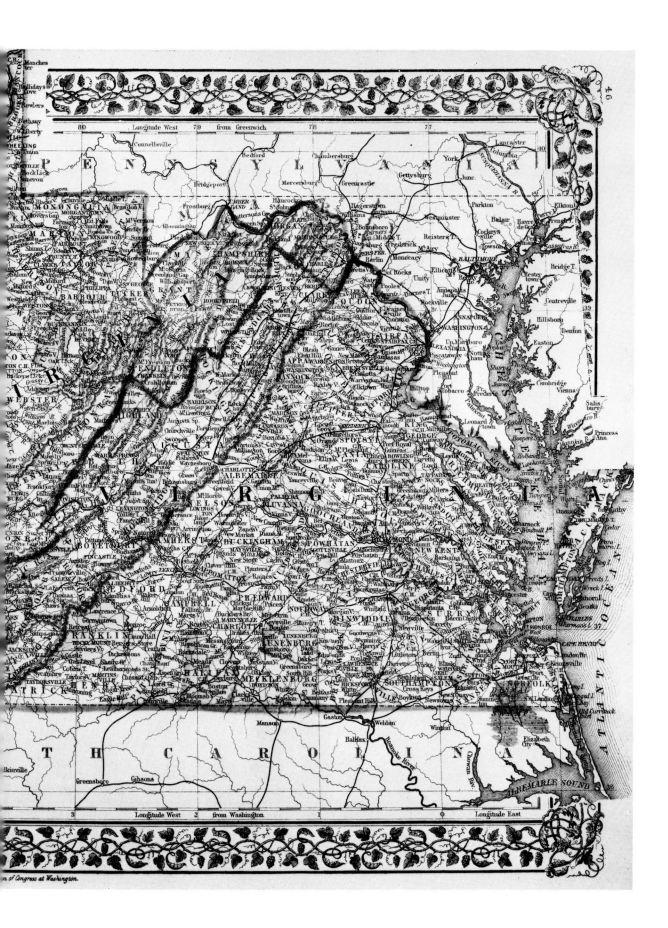

VIRGINIA

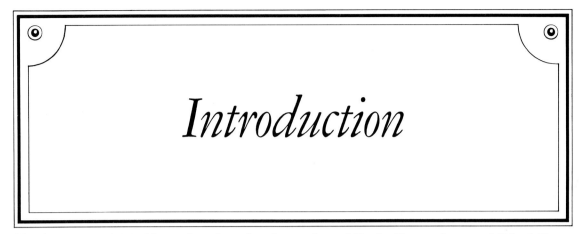

Introduction

The key to Virginia's history is a love for the land—for land and for the power which it confers on men and nations.

It was a desire for land that brought the first 104 settlers across the wintry Atlantic from London to Jamestown in 1607. It was land hunger that sent colonial Virginians westward and southward into the Indian country which became Kentucky, Tennessee, and the Carolinas. Spurred by this passion, Virginians for two centuries led America's westward surge: Alexander Spotswood, Dr. Thomas Walker, Daniel Boone, George Rogers Clark, Sam Houston, "Bigfoot" Wallace, Meriwether Lewis, and William Clark. It was a Virginia president, Thomas Jefferson, who bought the Louisiana Territory from France, and another, John Tyler, who pushed through Congress the annexation of Texas. In more recent times, Virginian Jim Bridger led prospectors over the Oregon Trail, and Richard Evelyn Byrd, another Virginian, explored the North and South poles.

This passion for land was an inheritance of the Englishmen who planted this first successful overseas colony in the centuries-long race for empire between tiny England and much larger Spain and France. "I dream of a new English nation," wrote Sir Walter Raleigh in the reign of Elizabeth I, articulating the ambitions of the confident Elizabethans whose explorations changed the world. It was Raleigh, hot-blooded courtier and mystic, who named Virginia for his "Virgin Queen" and promoted the first efforts to settle the unknown land in the 1580s.

The lure of Virginia's fabled riches survived countless early disappointments for the English, while Spain was growing rich from the gold and silver of the Incas and Aztecs. "Go and subdue!"

exhorted England's poet laureate Michael Drayton in his "Ode to the Virginian Voyage" in 1606. "Britons, ye stay too long." In the same year, playwrights George Chapman and John Marston painted Virginia in *Eastward Ho!* as bursting with gold, silver, and complaisant Indian maidens. Shakespeare himself wrote of the "still-vex't Bermoothes" in *The Tempest* after a Virginia-bound ship had been wrecked there in 1609. The poet-preacher John Donne, delivering a sermon to the Virginia Company at St. Paul's Church in London in 1621, praised the noble speculators and London guilds whose investment had made Virginia's settlement possible. Thus the name and fame of Virginia spread.

But the settlers themselves were the true heroes of England's first overseas empire. From farms, villages, and London streets they boarded tiny ships and huddled in stinking belowdeck quarters for the terrifying four-month voyage. Many ships faltered or foundered en route, but the arrival of the *Susan Constant, Godspeed,* and *Discovery* at the site named "James Towne" on May 13, 1607, showed that their ambitions could indeed be realized. At last England had a foothold in the New World. The tide of events was beginning to turn for the scepter'd isle and for North America as well. The era of Anglo-American dominance in world affairs was dawning.

Success did not come easily, however. The story of Virginia's first century is one of misplaced hope, naïveté, and misgovernment; but England muddled through. A few figures stand out heroically against the gloom: John Smith, Pocahontas, John Rolfe, the Reverend Robert Hunt, and Governor Sir George Yeardley, who brought the Great Charter of Rights and Privileges from London in 1618 and convened the first representative body in the New World—the Virginia Assembly—the next year.

Although the Virginia Company's charters of 1606 and 1609 designated most of the Atlantic seaboard between Florida and Canada as "Virginia," the settlement of Massachusetts in 1620 began the gradual diminution of that lordly empire. By 1681 five other colonies had been cut from her claimed bounds. Yet Virginia's head start kept her well in the lead among England's New World colonies. Of their approximately one hundred fifty thousand inhabitants in 1685, about seventy thousand lived in Virginia, compared with forty-eight thousand in Massachusetts and twenty thousand each in New York and Maryland. Much of Virginia's leadership in early America derived from her dominant size (until the cession of her Ohio Valley claims in 1784) and her dominant population, which was not to be equaled until New York at last overtook her in the census of 1820.

In the Jamestown century, Virginia developed a personality that long persisted: agrarian, easygoing, friendly, old-fashioned, pleasure-loving, conventional, slow to arouse, moderate in religious matters, fond of privacy, and respectful of precedent. Unlike the theocratic Puritans and dissenters of New England, the first English settlers of Virginia were conventional Anglicans. The "new English nation" begun at Jamestown followed in many ways the old one left behind at the dock on the Thames. Virginians took pride in their Englishness. The old-fashioned country squire of Fielding's *Tom Jones,* with his crops and horses and hounds, was the counterpart of Virginians from William Byrd I (1652–1704) to Harry Byrd I (1887–1966).

Three circumstances shaped the plantation economy that early grew along the James, York, and Potomac rivers: the emergence of tobacco, after 1612 Virginia's lifeblood, produced a rural economy that spread rapidly over Virginia's rich coastal plateau; interlacing waterways became the colony's natural highways, resulting in a thin-spread population and a strong dependence on local government; and Negro slavery offered the cheap labor that tobacco cultivation demanded, making possible the wealth and leisure that would produce the next century's Golden Age—and creating vast problems for the future.

Devoted as Virginia was to England, there were hints of adolescent disaffection from Jamestown as early as 1660. When Charles II ascended the throne at the end of the Puritan interregnum, he ungratefully refused Virginia's request that he rescind the hated Navigation Act (which forced Virginians to transport their tobacco only in English ships), although he acknowledged Virginia's loyalty by dubbing her his "Old Dominion." Rebellion flared in 1676 when the young activist Nathaniel Bacon objected that old Governor Sir William Berkeley had failed to protect frontier settlers against Indians. Bacon's Rebellion was an omen of events to come a century later.

The birth of a native Virginia opposition to His Majesty's government—a sign of increasing maturity—marked the clear emergence of a powerful planter class in Berkeley's governorship. Strengthening the "ancient planters" in these years was a large influx from England that included a number of King Charles II's Cavalier adherents who fled to Virginia to escape Cromwell's axmen. These ambitious colonials, who have been called the "Founders" of Virginia's greatness, created a power that partly counterbalanced the awesome weight of the royal governor. Tough, avaricious, and sometimes unscrupulous, they anticipated the Robber Barons of nineteenth-century America. Such were Robert "King" Carter of Lancaster County, William Byrd I of Charles City, Thomas Lee of Westmoreland, Philip Ludwell I of James City, and Benjamin Harrison II of Surry, among others. Later they were to be dignified as "first families" of Virginia.

As the Jamestown century neared its end, England's Glorious Revolution in 1688 brought King William and Queen Mary to the throne and relaxed England's policies toward dissenters and toward the colonies. Virginia took advantage of this to strengthen its church and to found a college to implant theological and intellectual development in its provincial society. The agent for these changes was a Scottish immigrant, the Reverend James Blair, who was named Virginia's representative of the bishop of London in 1689. It was Blair—as tough and almost as avaricious as his fellow "Founders"—who obtained a charter for the College of William and Mary from Their Majesties in 1693.

After a long and difficult childhood, Virginia was beginning to mature.

Jamestown's century was a time for planting; Williamsburg's was a period of cultivation and fast growth. The first settlement on the James had never grown large, and when fire gutted Jamestown's fourth statehouse in 1698, the Virginia Assembly heeded the advice of Governor Francis Nicholson and, after considering several sites for a new capital, settled on Middle Plantation, midway between the James and the York, where the College of William and Mary was already laid out. Renamed Williamsburg for King William III, the crossroads hamlet was created under Nicholson's guidance, with a mile-long central avenue extending from the college to the future capitol site. Nicholson named the axial street Duke of Gloucester for the young son of Princess Anne—later Queen Anne—and dubbed the others Francis, Nicholson, Scotland, Ireland, and Nassau.

The eighty years of Williamsburg's dominance were a happy era in Virginia's life. The little town grew to be the heart of an empire stretching from Chesapeake Bay to the region of the present state of Illinois. In these short years, Virginia expanded from a colony of some ninety thousand people to a commonwealth of nearly seven hundred fifty thousand. Proudly, Virginia emblazoned the motto *"En dat Virginia Quintum"* —"Behold, Virginia gives the fifth [Kingdom]" —ranking herself with the king's other claimed dominions, England, Scotland, Ireland, and France.

This growth was part of the mercantilist upsurge which eventually was to make Britain the greatest empire in world history. Protected by an unsurpassed navy and merchant marine, British trade outgrew all competition. Virginia tobacco, grain, and lumber traveled to the farthest parts of the globe. In return, Virginia planters and farmers bought manufactured goods from the British Isles, rum and sugar from the West Indies, and slaves from British ships trading with Africa. Rome in its heyday never grew as great as Britain had become.

Despite British efforts to force Virginians to trade through a few central ports, eighteenth-century Virginia remained rural—"a sylvan Venice," one writer called it—except for such villages as Yorktown, Hampton, Norfolk, Fredericksburg, Richmond, Petersburg, Falmouth, Port Royal, and Alexandria. Each autumn, ships called at dozens of planters' docks and tobacco inspection warehouses along tidal rivers, loaded the wooden hogsheads packed with tobacco, and, when fully laden, gathered at anchorages in lower Chesapeake Bay to await the transatlantic sailing of the tobacco fleet.

After Parliament passed the Act of Union in 1707, Scotland's improved status drew much of Virginia's trade away from London and Bristol to the Scottish ports of Aberdeen and Glasgow. Despite the protection of British warships—the admiral sailing in the lead ship and the rear admiral in the wake—convoys were often attacked by enemy ships during the eighteenth century's frequent wars. Come spring, the surviving ships returned from Britain to Virginia, often by way of the West Indies, this time bearing the goods ordered by individual planters or by Virginia shopkeepers and traveling peddlers.

The rise of Williamsburg in these years reflected the rise of London as a center of trade, government, intellectual affairs, and the arts. Williamsburg became a center of social life for lowland Virginia, even though its year-round population did not exceed two thousand souls. The "great planter" class arose in these years and tightened its hold on the remunerative offices and political honors of the colony. Such families as the Pages, Burwells, Hills, Cockes, and Randolphs bought and bred slaves to produce their tobacco. With the profits they built great houses like Rosewell, Carter's Grove, Shirley, Mount Pleasant, and Wilton.

The eighteenth-century world was still close enough to the Middle Ages to suffer from much of the class consciousness, religious intolerance, superstition, and racial feeling of that benighted era. In this stratified society, slavery did not seem the great evil that it was. Thus Virginia, in common with other agrarian colonies, developed an economy based on slave labor. As the serfs of feudal Europe had done, slaves made possible in Virginia a wealthy, semileisured class which was able to devote time to pleasure: to reading, study, philosophy, the arts, and writing as well as to gambling, the chase, dancing, drinking, hunting, and social gaiety.

In the beginning only a few prescient souls acknowledged the injustice of such a social order. It was the tragic irony of Virginia's history that a system that enslaved blacks and drove many able middle-class white people out of Virginia in search of opportunity should simultaneously have produced the greatest galaxy of political talent in the Western world since the Athens of Pericles.

Yet such was the case. In eighteenth-century Virginia, young men on rural plantations read Plato, Aristotle, John Locke, Montesquieu, and Adam Smith in search of the good society. At the College of William and Mary, the enlightenment of the Age of Reason manifested itself to young Thomas Jefferson, Edmund Randolph, James Monroe, and others of their generation. Within a hundred years, these grandsons and great-grandsons of the Founders would help create a more democratic America. As Vernon Louis Parrington wrote in *The Romantic Revolution in America:* "Between the older colonial America and later industrial America stand the ideals of the Old Dominion, more humane and generous than either, disseminating the principles of French romantic philosophy and instilling into the provincial American mind, static and stagnant in the grip of English colonization, the ideal of democratic equalitarianism and the hope of humane progress. The nineteenth century first entered America by way of the James River."

Dumas Malone called revolutionary Virginians "the Great Generation," but their lives actually spanned the 115 years from 1721, when Peyton Randolph was born in Williamsburg, until 1836, when James Madison died at Montpelier. Jefferson was their apotheosis. Born an aristocrat but philosophically a democrat, he embodied many Virginia ideals that persist into the classless twentieth century.

Jefferson shared the love of science that made naturalists of such Virginians as John Clayton, John Custis, Mark Catesby, and John Banister. He was versed in philosophy like William Byrd II, Richard Bland, James Madison, and Governor Francis Fauquier. He felt the passion for the law that motivated his teacher, George Wythe, as well as Edmund Pendleton, St. George Tucker, John Marshall, and John Taylor of Caroline. Like many of his contemporaries—John Randolph the Tory, William Short, James Monroe, Joseph Carrington Cabell—he loved architecture and the arts. Finally, he shared the deistic views of many of his Virginia contemporaries—another irony in the Anglican world of Virginia.

In at least two respects, though, Jefferson was less typical of the Virginia of his time; he had little interest in field sports or in military life. In these matters George Washington was more representative of the Virginia squirearchy. They made him "first in war, first in peace, and first in the hearts of his countrymen," as Washington's friend and fellow Virginian General Henry "Lighthorse Harry" Lee wrote.

How did it happen that Virginia, which so greatly admired and emulated Mother England, should have taken the lead in resisting the Stamp Act and other British severities of the 1760s and 1770s? Why should Virginia have been the first of the thirteen colonies in 1765 to speak out in the voice of Patrick Henry: "Caesar had his Brutus, Charles I his Cromwell, and George III . . ."—here Henry was interrupted by cries of "Treason! Treason!"—"and George III may profit by their example. If this be treason, make the most of it!"?

Part of it was due to the liberating effects on Virginia of the Age of Reason. Part was the anti-English bias of Scotch-Irish newcomers who swelled Virginia's population after 1720. Also a cause was Virginia's long resentment of imperialist policies which placed tobacco growers at the mercy of British shippers and buyers. In the final analysis, however, the debates that shook the House of Burgesses from 1765 onward reflected the fury of an Old Dominion that treasured its British rights and felt itself betrayed by a king and a ministry insensitive to them.

Thus, after years of growth and groping, the colony of Virginia by 1776 had achieved the confidence to propose independence from Britain. The day of decision came on May 15, 1776, when the Virginia Convention in Williamsburg unanimously voted to petition the Continental Congress in Philadelphia to declare the thirteen colonies free and independent states. On June 7 in Philadelphia, Richard Henry Lee of Westmoreland County introduced the motion. The result was the Declaration of Independence, penned largely by Thomas Jefferson and officially adopted by Congress on July 4, 1776. It was a fateful step. Virginia had indeed come a long way since May 13, 1607.

Throughout its first century, Virginia remained largely English, except for slaves. However, its second hundred years brought new streams which diversified—and ultimately democratized and enriched—the prevailing patterns along the coastal plain called Tidewater. The fall line of the rivers that empty into Chesapeake Bay served for many years after 1607 as a barrier to inland settlement; but in time masses of immigrants inexorably moved westward, crossing the fall line of the great rivers at villages that eventually grew to be Richmond, Petersburg, Fredericksburg, and Falmouth.

One notable move into the uplands occurred in 1700, when 207 Huguenot immigrants settled on the James River, ten miles above the fall line, in what became Goochland County. With the Reverend Benjamin de Joux, a Frenchman of Anglican ordination, as their leader, they cleared and occupied land made available to them by William Byrd II and formerly occupied by the Monacan Indians. Many other Huguenot families settled Virginia in these years—Maurys, Fontaines, Seviers, Letchers, Dabneys, Moncures, Latanés—contributing greatly to the life of the commonwealth.

Another inland thrust was made in 1716, when Governor Alexander Spotswood led sixty-two horsemen westward from Williamsburg to the heights of the Blue Ridge Mountains to see what lay beyond them. As successor to Governor Nicholson, Colonel Spotswood shared his zeal for Britain's spreading empire. But Spotswood also understood the concern of Virginians over rival French ambitions in the Ohio Valley, west of Virginia. He knew that Louis XIV had sent settlers into the Mississippi region to claim the interior of North America, establishing a fort on the Gulf of Mexico and claiming the Mississippi River and all lands drained by its tributaries. If Virginia did not seize and hold her claimed Ohio Valley lands before France did, Great Britain might lose that strategic area.

Spotswood spent his last six years as Virginia's governor allying the upland Indians with the colony and strengthening the Virginia frontier. To that end, he promoted a conference at Albany, New York, in 1722 between chiefs of the Five Nations and the English governors of New York, Pennsylvania, and Virginia. There, after many gifts, libations, and toasts, the English persuaded the Iroquois chiefs to sign a treaty not to come into Virginia east of the Blue Ridge or south of the Potomac River. In return, Virginia agreed to allow the Iroquois continued use of their ancient north-south Warriors' Path through the Valley of Virginia. (This concession was later bought back from the Indians through the Treaty of Lancaster, Pennsylvania, in 1744, as settlement of Virginia's uplands continued to surge westward.)

The Iroquois addressed Virginians at these treaty gatherings as "*Assaragoa,*" an Indian word meaning "long knife." This was because Virginia's governor at the first Iroquois negotiations, held at Albany in 1685, had been Lord Howard of Effingham, whose name resembled the Dutch word *howar* or "long knife." The Dutch interpreter accordingly dubbed Governor Howard "Assaragoa," a name that stuck to his successors. Virginians continued to be "long knives" to Indians throughout colonial times.

Thanks to Spotswood, Virginia's policy after 1716 was to befriend frontier Indians and encourage settlement of western Virginia. From Pennsylvania and Maryland, a few Germanic immigrants began to cross the upper Potomac as early as 1726, led by Jacob Stover. More Germans and Swiss came in 1732, when Joist Hite, who had first farmed in Pennsylvania, led fellow Alsatians to settle on forty thousand acres in upland Virginia which the governor had granted to John and Isaac Van Meter. Soon the upper valley was alive with Germanic immigrants from Alsace, Switzerland, and the Rhenish Palatinate, all seeking cheap farmland and the opportunity to live and worship peaceably. In the group were Lutherans, Amish, Dunkers, German Baptists, Mennonites, and other Protestants.

Close on their heels came a wave of Scotch-Irish immigrants. More numerous and assertive than the Germans, they rapidly dominated northern Virginia. Goaded by Anglican religious laws and English landlords in Northern Ireland, these Ulster Scots had crossed the Atlantic in order to enjoy the religious freedom of William Penn's Pennsylvania, only to find that the best lands there had already been taken. Before descending into Virginia, however, these disciples of John Knox inquired of Governor William Gooch in 1738 what "civil and religious liberties" they would enjoy in that Anglican hotbed. Gooch's reply indicates the growth of toleration in Virginia. The governor said he had "always been inclined to favour the people who have lately removed from other provinces, to settle on the western side of our great mountains. . . . No interruption shall be given to any minister of your profession [denomination] who shall come among them, so long as they conform themselves to the rules prescribed by the act of toleration in

England, by taking the oaths enjoined thereby, and registering the places of their meeting, and behave peaceably towards the government. . . ."

As Spotswood had foreseen, the conflict of French and Virginian claims to the Ohio Valley soon led to war. By 1750, French forces from Canada were moving into the Ohio area, prompting Governor Robert Dinwiddie in 1754 to send a force under Major George Washington from Winchester to the French outpost at Fort Duquesne, at the present site of Pittsburgh. When Washington's small force was compelled to retreat, England sent out Major General Edward Braddock with a larger detachment. In a bloody battle in 1755, Braddock's force was defeated, and he was mortally wounded. For the next three years, then, uncontrolled Indian attacks terrorized Virginia's frontier. But a new campaign finally brought victory; English regulars under General John Forbes and Virginia militiamen under Washington at last occupied Fort Duquesne on November 25, 1758.

The French having been expelled, Virginia settlers again moved westward toward the Ohio until the British in 1763 forbade settlement west of the Alleghenies. Although designed to avert further war with the Indians, the crown's proclamation was resented in Virginia, where thousands of citizen soldiers had received western grants in payment for their service in the French and Indian Wars. In spite of the edict, migrations toward the Ohio continued.

The main Virginia artery to the west and the south in this period was the Indians' former Warriors' Path, which had grown by 1750 into a wagon road extending the full length of the Valley of Virginia. At Big Lick, later renamed Roanoke, one branch of the road ran south to the Carolinas and the other led westward to the Kentucky and Tennessee territories. Shown on the 1775 edition of Joshua Fry and Peter Jefferson's map of Virginia as "The Great Wagon Road from the Yadkin River through Virginia to Philadelphia, distant 435 miles," the artery carried a stream of emigrants southward to the Carolinas, Georgia, and adjoining lands. Wrote the historian Carl Bridenbaugh: "In the last sixteen years of the colonial era, southbound traffic along the Great Philadelphia Wagon Road was numbered in tens of thousands; it was the most heavily traveled road in all America and must have had more vehicles jolting along its rough and tortuous

way than all other main roads put together."

At the western end of the Valley of Virginia, early emigrants created settlements along the Holston, New, Nolichucky, and Clinch rivers. Access over the rocky Cumberland Mountains into Kentucky was almost impossible until Daniel Boone in 1775 cut a narrow horse path through the thick vegetation, creating the Wilderness Road which led more than seventy thousand people into "Caintuck" by the time Kentucky became the fifteenth state in 1792. Thus began the proliferation of settlements in the Ohio Valley, which was to make Virginia the "Mother of States and of Statesmen."

The contrasts between eastern and western Virginians were marked. To the settled English descendants of Tidewater, the new Scotch-Irish and Germanic settlers of the west seemed uncouth. Tidewatermen called the upland Scots "Cohees" for their locution "Quoth he." Uplanders in turn derided lowlanders as "Tuckahoes" for their fondness for eating swamp root, called "tuckahoe" by Indians. Frontier Scots accused Virginia's government of sacrificing them to the Indians during decades of border warfare. True or not, the Covenanters proved skilled fighters, joining other hillmen from Kentucky, Tennessee, and the Carolinas to fight revolutionary battles at King's Mountain, Cowpens, Guilford Courthouse, Salisbury, and Camden. Their Appalachian life made them brave, hardy, and resilient.

The Germanic frontiersman was less feisty, but he had other virtues. Germans made *jaeger* or "hunter" rifles which evolved into the Pennsylvania and Kentucky rifles—deadly weapons in the hands of western soldiers in the Revolution. Germanic wagoners hauled guns, food, and wounded soldiers in their Conestoga-style wagons. Many Germans proved good fighters. The most celebrated was tall, rawboned Peter Muhlenberg, a Lutheran minister at Woodstock, who cast off his clerical robe after a sermon in 1776 to reveal his militia uniform beneath. "I am a clergyman, it is true," he told his congregation, "but I am a member of society, as well as the poorest layman. My liberty is as dear to me as to any man. Shall I, then, sit still and enjoy myself at home when the best blood of the continent is spilling? Heaven forbid it!" With that, he was off to war, and by the time of the siege of Yorktown in 1781, he had risen to the rank of general.

In the fierce sectionalism of early Virginia were

hints of a civil war and of the split of one state into two. Yet it was perhaps an inevitable stage in the ethnic and cultural interplay that would ultimately produce a more pluralistic, democratic, and tolerant union. From the elitism of Tidewater and the egalitarianism of Appalachia would come a consensus such as was expressed in the election of a William Henry Harrison, a John Tyler, a Zachary Taylor, and a Woodrow Wilson—Virginians all. But first struggle had to come.

Throughout the eighteenth century, Virginia was increasingly outspoken on behalf of what she considered her citizens' rights. Governor Spotswood complained of Virginians in 1716, "By their professions and actions, they seem to allow no jurisdiction, civil or ecclesiastical, but what is established by laws of their own making." From the time of Patrick Henry's Stamp Act resolutions in 1765 onward, Virginians took a lead. Their Committee of Correspondence, led by Henry, Jefferson, Dabney Carr, and the Lee brothers— Richard Henry and Francis Lightfoot—was preparing for the coming break with Britain. "Oh, those Virginians are noble spirits," wrote Oxenbridge Thacher of Boston in 1765.

When the First Continental Congress met at Philadelphia in 1774, Peyton Randolph of Williamsburg was named president. If any doubt of Virginia's position remained, Patrick Henry soon dispelled it with his demand before the Virginia Convention of 1775: "Give me liberty or give me death!" Alarmed by the spreading rebellion, Virginia's Governor Dunmore moved the colony's gunpowder from the public magazine in Williamsburg, but the act only increased popular fury and determination. Less than two months later, the harassed Dunmore fled Williamsburg and took refuge aboard a British man-of-war. At the same time, in Philadelphia, George Washington was chosen by the Second Continental Congress as commander of the Continental Army. Virginia—Britain's first overseas colony—had left the empire.

The revolution in Virginia's government was rapid. An eleven-member Committee of Safety governed for a year while Dunmore sought from his shipboard command post to raise a supporting force of loyalists and freed slaves. At first entrenching himself at Norfolk, the governor was forced to flee that port in December 1775, after his forces were beaten by Virginia and North Carolina militia in the battle of Great Bridge. Norfolk itself was burned by the patriots on January 1, 1776, in order to destroy loyalist property there. In the summer of 1776, Dunmore gave up his hopeless fight and left Virginia after his defeat by General Andrew Lewis's militia in the battle of Gwynn's Island.

The new Commonwealth of Virginia was created by a convention of 120 men who met for sixty days in Williamsburg, from May 6 through July 5, 1776. Reiterating Virginia's faith in law, the founders first approved a declaration of rights offered by George Mason. In the same month it adopted a constitution. The new government showed the effect of John Locke and England's Glorious Revolution by giving dominance to the General Assembly and subordinating the governorship, which was to be filled by annual vote of the Assembly. Patrick Henry was elected to that office.

The most momentous enactment of the 1776 convention was the resolution calling on the Continental Congress to declare "that these United Colonies are and of right ought to be, free and independent States, and that a plan of confederation be submitted to the several colonies." Taken to Philadelphia by dispatch riders, it was introduced by Richard Henry Lee into the Continental Congress on June 7, 1776. It was adopted, and a committee was named to prepare a document. Committee member John Adams called on Thomas Jefferson, then thirty-three, to prepare the Declaration of Independence. "It is fitting for a Virginian to be at the head of this business," Adams said, and the congress evidently agreed.

British hostilities in the war's first years were directed chiefly at Boston, New York, and other northern ports. To repel these attacks, most of Virginia's troops were sent north. However, Governor Henry in 1778 secretly dispatched 150 militiamen under George Rogers Clark to surprise British garrisons on the Ohio River and seize control of Virginia's claimed Northwest Territory. In frontier battles at Kaskaskia and Cahokia, Illinois, and at Vincennes, Indiana, Clark's men defeated the British. Governor Sir Henry Hamilton was captured and returned to Williamsburg, and Virginia's claims to the Ohio lands were held for the new nation. From them ultimately were formed the states of Ohio, Indiana, Illinois, Michigan, and Wisconsin.

In 1780 the Revolution moved into Virginia.

British forces under Generals Cornwallis, Phillips, and Benedict Arnold scoured Tidewater, while the cavalrymen of Colonel Banastre Tarleton pursued Governor Jefferson to Monticello and the General Assembly to Staunton. Forewarned by Jack Jouett, who rode at night from Louisa County to warn the legislators of Tarleton's approach, most of them avoided capture.

Cornwallis's object in Virginia was to shatter its military power and thus split the northern colonies from the southern. "I was most fully persuaded," he later wrote, "that, until Virginia was reduced, we could not hold the more southern provinces, and that after its reduction, they could fall without more difficulty." But Cornwallis had not reckoned with America's newfound ally, France. Cut off from naval support by the victory of a French fleet over British ships off the Virginia capes on September 5, 1781, Cornwallis was forced to surrender his army of seventy-five hundred men at Yorktown on October 19. Revolutionary combat came to a virtual end. A few years later, in 1783, American independence was recognized by the Treaty of Paris.

In many other fields of action besides the political, Virginians distinguished themselves in the Revolution. John Paul Jones raided British shores in the *Bonhomme Richard* in 1778 and sank H.M.S. *Serapis* in 1779, Arthur Lee served with Benjamin Franklin and Silas Deane in negotiating the French alliance in 1778; Daniel Morgan, "Lighthorse Harry" Lee, William Campbell, and others were effective generals; and Thomas Whiting, James and Richard Barron, John Sinclair, and other seafaring men—many of them black crew members—supplied Virginia troops with guns and ammunition brought from the West Indies throughout the war, in defiance of British coastal blockades. Numerous other Virginians served as wagon drivers, gunsmiths, iron and lead miners, millers, cooks, blacksmiths, and dispatch riders; all were essential to victory.

War is a young man's game, but the drafting of the constitution needs seasoned heads. To the Constitutional Convention at Philadelphia in 1787 Virginia sent seven of her leading men: Washington, Mason, Wythe, Madison, Edmund Randolph, John Blair II, and Dr. James McClurg. (Jefferson was serving as minister to France, and Patrick Henry, skeptical of all government, "smelt a rat.") Despite Virginia's initiative in the Revolution, her convention of 1788, called to ratify the Constitution, bitterly assailed the compromise document and at last approved it by a vote of only eighty-nine to seventy-nine. Among those arrayed against it were Mason, Henry, James Monroe, Benjamin Harrison, and Judge John Tyler—the latter two both fathers of presidents-to-be. The Constitution's proponents were led by Madison, Randolph, John Marshall, and Henry "Lighthorse Harry" Lee.

Only Madison's promise to offer a bill of rights as early amendments to the Constitution, Jefferson's written assurances of support from Paris, and Washington's quoted endorsement, "I am fully persuaded . . . that it [ratification] or disunion is before us," carried the day for federal union. Even so, the convention added this proviso:

We, the delegates of the people of Virginia . . . do, in the name and in behalf of the People of Virginia, declare and make known, that the powers granted under the Constitution, being derived from the people of the United States, may be resumed by them whensoever the same shall be perverted to their injury or oppression, and that every power not granted thereby remains with them and at their will; that therefore no right of any denomination can be cancelled, abridged, restrained, or modified by the Congress . . . or any department of or officer of the United States, except in those instances in which power is given by the Constitution for those purposes; and that, among other essential rights, the liberty of conscience and of the press cannot be cancelled, abridged, restrained, or modified by any authority of the United States.

Thus Virginia declared herself unequivocally for strict construction of the Constitution. It was a viewpoint that she retained in the centuries to come.

Yet with power so great, what did Virginians fear? While Patrick Henry was direfully predicting northern domination and southern decline, a handsome new Virginia capitol was rising nearby on Richmond's Capitol Hill. Around it loomed a commonwealth grown to 747,000 people, stretching from the Virginia capes to the Ohio Valley. To link western Virginia with the east, plans were then afoot to connect the Kanawha River by canal to the James, bringing western produce to the growing port cities of Richmond, Petersburg, and Norfolk. Advocates of the plans saw unlimited markets for Virginia's farm crops, lumber, furs, and coal. She would dominate the union, they argued, not suffer from it.

This optimistic view was at first confirmed by events. Until the commercialization of the North revolutionized nineteenth-century America, "the sceptre of Virginia" continued to prevail. Washington, Jefferson, Madison, and Monroe served successively as president, with only John Adams in 1797–1801 to interrupt the dynasty. Of the four members of his first cabinet President Washington chose two from Virginia: Jefferson and Edmund Randolph. Five of the first seven secretaries of state were from the Old Dominion, as were the lion's share of territorial governors.

To protect the states' rights, Jefferson and Madison insisted that the Constitution made the states "co-equals" of the nation in all except foreign affairs. When John Adams became president in 1797, Virginia's strict constructionists saw hope of limiting central power by allying northern workingmen with southern farmers. Slowly, by pen and persuasion, Jefferson and his states' righters developed the Democratic-Republican party to counteract the centralism of Adams, Hamilton, and John Marshall, who in 1801 became chief justice of the United States Supreme Court. The contest between Federalists —precursors of today's Republicans—and the Jeffersonians—later called Democrats—was enacted against the backdrop of early Washington, D.C., which in 1800 became the nation's capital, on a Potomac River site given by Virginia and Maryland.

Simultaneous with the rise of parties was the birth of an increasingly virulent sectionalism— at first between North and South and later between East and West. These flames were fed by President Adams's ill-conceived Alien and Sedition Acts of 1798, which infringed the Constitution by subjecting newspaper critics of government to libel charges and by restricting press freedom. Jefferson in the same year secretly encouraged Kentucky's legislature to declare the acts "void and of no effect" and to assert a state's right to reject them. Madison obtained passage by Virginia's Assembly of similar resolutions urging states to join "in maintaining unimpaired the authority, rights and liberties" reserved to them. Already the Union was in jeopardy.

As Virginia's new capital, Richmond acquired the luster that was once Williamsburg's. Built in the neoclassic style, it sat serenely atop hills overlooking the James and its canal, where docks and warehouses received cargo from the up-country. In the same period, the ports of Norfolk, Petersburg, Alexandria, and Lynchburg also throve, overcoming the early lead of Jamestown, Williamsburg, Yorktown, Port Royal, and Falmouth. The center of Virginia's power was shifting from Tidewater to Piedmont.

Yet eastern Virginia continued to be an important arena, from the time of the Constitution's ratification in 1788 until John Quincy Adams's election as president ended the reign of Virginia's dynasty in 1825. Thomas Ritchie's powerful *Richmond Enquirer* spread Jeffersonian dogma throughout the nation, rebutted fiercely by John Hampden Pleasants's *Richmond Whig;* their rivalry led to a duel in which Ritchie's son killed Pleasants. Under brilliant Chief Justice Spencer Roane, Virginia's Supreme Court asserted its "co-equality" with the nation's. And when Marshall's court rejected Virginia court decisions on grounds of error, Roane and each of his associates wrote opinions declining to reexamine the cases. The Virginia Assembly objected that John Marshall had created "a centripetal force" that threatened to vitiate the necessary "centrifugal force" of the states. The contest between Jeffersonians and Federalists reached its apogee with the trial of Aaron Burr for treason in Richmond in 1807, when Chief Justice Marshall issued a subpoena for President Jefferson's appearance. Precedents were set for years to come.

An insight into Virginia at this period was provided by William Ellery Channing when he came from Harvard to tutor the children of David Meade Randolph: "Here I find great vices but greater virtues. There is one single trait that attaches me . . . more than all the virtues of New England. They *love money less* than we do. They are more disinterested. . . . Could I only take from Virginians their sensuality and their slaves, I should think them the greatest people in the world."

It was a refrain to be heard increasingly in the years that led up to Fort Sumter.

America's political climate changed clearly in the 1820–21 struggle leading to the Missouri Compromise. To most Virginians who were slaveholders, abolitionist effort to exclude slavery from the Louisiana Territory states was another usurpation of states' rights by the aggressive North. Jefferson, who by 1820 had become an elder statesman, likened the issue to "a fire bell in the night." John Randolph of Roanoke was so incensed by the congressional debate over Missouri's admission that for days he could eat only gruel and crackers. Though the compromise ultimately permitted slavery in states south of latitude 30°30′N, the "peculiar institution" and the South that practiced it were now to be increasingly under abolitionist pressure.

Virginia's old-fashioned hierarchical society was assailed in other ways, too. In the census of 1820 she lost population supremacy for the first time to New York, whose Erie Canal was being dug to deliver the commerce of the Great Lakes to Manhattan. Slavery discouraged European immigrants from coming south, impelling them instead to the North and West. Ambitious men, who might have prospered in the fluid society of seventeenth-century Tidewater, found fewer chances in the fixed society that had developed by the nineteenth. Many of them went west through Cumberland Gap or south over the Great Wagon Road. Virginia was the Southwest's seedbed. "All the young men are going west," complained a Virginia lady; and it was almost true.

The exodus was but another chapter in the pilgrimage of Western man. Since Elizabethan times, a ferment of ambitions and faiths had thrust Europeans across the Atlantic in search of Utopia. Jamestown and Plymouth were stepping-stones to the Ohio, the Mississippi, and ultimately to the Pacific. Often the best men chose to move on: William Henry Harrison from Charles City County to Ohio; Henry Clay from Hanover County to Kentucky; John Sevier from Rockingham County to Tennessee; William H. Crawford from Nelson County to Georgia; Sam Houston from Rockbridge County to Texas; Cyrus McCormick from Rockbridge to Illinois— the list is long. In the 150 years after 1774, at least 329 men who represented other states in Congress had been born in Virginia.

Tension over slavery increased sectionalism within Virginia. Westerners complained that the Assembly in Richmond failed to provide western roads and canals. True, the James and Potomac had been canalized, but capital—or was it will? —was lacking to push the work beyond the Appalachians. Virginia's one-dimensional economy had been handicapped for lack of currency since 1607; its cumbersome exchange was based

largely on barter and on receipts for land, slaves, and tobacco. Perhaps Richmond was the capital of eastern Virginia, uplanders sometimes said; as for them, they looked to the government in Washington.

These differences were argued effectively for the first time at a constitutional convention in Richmond in 1829. Called "the Last Meeting of the Giants," it drew among its delegates Madison, Monroe, Marshall, and Randolph of Roanoke. Though the west won a few concessions, the east kept its disproportionate electoral power by virtue of its slaves, who formed a third of the population east of the Blue Ridge. But long after 1829, the dominantly eastern Assembly continued to dictate the selection of a governor, who was advised by a twelve-man Council of State, also dominantly eastern.

Of Virginia's forty-one governors from 1776 to 1861, all but eight came from east of the Blue Ridge. When Jefferson's Republicans split in the 1832 presidential election, Virginians were badly divided. Easterners favored the polished Henry Clay, while westerners supported hickory-cured Andrew Jackson. Two Virginias were emerging, based on divergent interests.

Despite such dissension, Virginia experienced a growth of the arts and of education in the mid-nineteenth century. At Jefferson's behest, the state created a progressive university at Charlottesville in 1825. However, the church continued for another century to be the chief agency of higher learning, as it had been since the Middle Ages. A Presbyterian academy, started in 1749 in Augusta County, grew into Washington College in 1816; Presbyterians also opened Hampden-Sydney College in 1776. Methodists founded Randolph-Macon College at Boydton in 1830, and Baptists sowed the seeds for the University of Richmond in 1840. The Medical College of Virginia began as an offshoot of Hampden-Sydney in 1837, and Virginia Military Institute was created two years later. Many sectarian academies, seminaries, and institutes were born in this era, most of them absorbed into the public school system after 1870.

A sprinkling of writers and poets appeared, though none except Edgar Allan Poe was of first rank. A native of Boston, Poe grew up in Richmond as the ward of John Allan, a wealthy merchant. Although he spent much of his creative life in the North, he returned to Richmond in 1835 to edit, for a short time, the *Southern Literary Messenger,* which became an influential journal. By and large, however, Virginia's writers suffered from the chivalric influence of Sir Walter Scott, a southern idol. Most of them lacked the vigor and directness of their northern contemporaries, although a few of them—William A. Caruthers, Nathaniel Beverley Tucker, Henry Ruffner, and John Esten Cooke—were widely read.

Much southern writing was flawed by its defense of slavery. To escape the worrisome present, Virginians looked back longingly to the plumed knights of *Ivanhoe* and the swooning ladies of *Kenilworth.* The literary image of Virginia's aristocratic "Cavalier" thus was born—an image in radiant contrast to the "Yankee" who meanly counted the shekels he gained from the slave trade while loudly demanding slavery's abolition.

A thin vein of abolitionist sentiment was evident in Virginia for a few years after 1776, when Jefferson, Wythe, and George Mason had proposed an end to slave trading. But outright abolition seemed impractical to the average Virginian. Various plans to free blacks were offered, and some freedmen were actually sent to the African state of Liberia in an effort backed by James Monroe, John Marshall, and others. A wider emancipation was at last debated in the 1831–32 Assembly. Then, suddenly, a band of slaves under Nat Turner rose up in Southampton County and killed nearly sixty people. Virginia thus lost its best chance to free itself of a doomed way of life. After 1832, the fear of freedmen and resentment of abolitionists fanned the talk of secession in Virginia, as they had earlier among cotton planters of the Deep South.

Virginia remained wedded to the Union, sustained by her pride in its creation and her faith in its laws, even after John Brown and his abolitionist followers seized the federal arsenal at Harper's Ferry in 1859. Brown, a fanatic, planned to arm the slaves and lead them in revolt, but they failed to rally around him. A force of Virginia militiamen and United States Marines under Lieutenant Colonel Robert E. Lee captured Brown, who was quickly tried for treason against Virginia, convicted, and executed.

In the embittered election of 1860, soon there-

after, a coalition of northerners and westerners elected Abraham Lincoln president. Almost immediately, seven states in the Deep South seceded and formed the Confederate States of America, with headquarters in Montgomery.

Virginia, the patient advocate of sectional compromise, doubled its efforts to preserve the Union. Meeting in Richmond in February 1861, the General Assembly proposed that all the states send delegates to a Washington conference to resolve the impasse. Ex-President John Tyler, then seventy, came out of retirement in Charles City to carry the plan to Lincoln, while Judge John Robertson of Petersburg was dispatched to South Carolina to urge restraint. But Virginia's "Peace Convention" could not avert the inevitable. Soon South Carolina's guns thundered their fury at Fort Sumter. Edmund Ruffin, a Virginia states' righter, fired the first shot. When Lincoln called for state troops to quell the rebellion, the hitherto divided Virginia Convention voted to secede. Virginia joined the Confederacy, and Richmond became capital of the "Rebellion."

Years later, Vernon Louis Parrington was to conclude in *The Romantic Revolution in America:* "Until the problem of slavery became acute, and leadership passed from moderate Virginians to fire-eaters from further south, the influence of Virginia at Washington was thrown on the side of republican simplicity, low taxes, and the decentralization of power. The armed clash over slavery very probably might have been averted if the spirit of the Old Dominion had prevailed."

It was a just verdict.

By seceding, Virginia doomed herself to be the arena of the war. As the northern frontier of the eleven-state Confederacy, she faced certain invasion. Outnumbered by a Union population of twenty-two million to the South's nine million and hopelessly outgunned by northern industry, Virginia and the South contemplated a lightning war to bring the troubled Lincoln to his knees. They hopefully invoked "Southern hot-headed dash, reckless gallantry, spirit of adventure," in the words of South Carolina's Wade Hampton. But it was not to be.

Robert E. Lee, who had declined General Winfield Scott's offer of command of the Union armies, resigned his federal commission to become the commander of Virginia's forces. "Trusting in almighty God, an approving conscience, and the aid of my fellow citizens," he said, "I devote myself to the service of my native State, in whose behalf alone will I ever again draw my sword."

Lee spoke for eastern Virginians but not for the trans-Appalachian western countries. Unappeased by the belated revision of the state constitution in 1851, they opposed Virginia's secession and, at a meeting in Wheeling a few months later, withdrew from the Old Dominion. By this act, which was legitimized by Congress in 1863, Virginia's population and expanse were both reduced by a third. From an original spread of 313,279 square miles before she entered the Union, the state was reduced in 1863 to 40,815 square miles and a million people. No longer could she vie with New York and Pennsylvania for leadership.

Confederate strategy was to carry the war to the North, while Lincoln's objective was to capture the Confederate capital at Richmond. The South's effort began promisingly in 1861 with a victory at Bull Run, thirty miles southwest of Washington; but follow-up Confederate forays into Maryland and Pennsylvania were repelled. After the bloody debacle of Gettysburg in 1863, the South's hopes slowly died.

Lee took field command of Virginia's chief army in 1862, after General Joseph E. Johnston was wounded at Seven Pines while fighting back General George B. McClellan's assault on Richmond in the Peninsula campaign. The genius of Lee and his "right hand," Stonewall Jackson, who immortalized himself in the Valley of Virginia campaign in 1862 before his fatal injury, were acclaimed throughout the world. The southern cause was especially popular in the British Isles, where kinship was felt with the plantation world. Besides Lee and Jackson, the names of many other Virginians were immortalized—among them James Ewell Brown ("Jeb") Stuart, Richard S. Ewell, Ambrose P. Hill, John Singleton Mosby, Turner Ashby, and Daniel Harvey Hill.

A few Virginians, unlike Lee, felt a stronger loyalty to the Union than to their native state. Two who chose thus were General George H. Thomas of Southampton County, who became known as the "Rock of Chickamauga" for his campaign in Tennessee, and Winfield Scott of Dinwiddie, one of the heroes of the Mexican War, who remained as chief of staff of the United States Army throughout most of the war.

The Union's overwhelming naval supremacy permitted its gunboats to claim and hold control of Virginia waterways throughout the war. However, this control was challenged in 1862 by the Confederate ironclad *Virginia*—originally the federal frigate *Merrimack*—which battled the Union's *Monitor* in Hampton Roads in 1862 while spectators watched from the Hampton and Norfolk shores. Neither vessel seriously hurt the other, but the battle introduced the age of armored ships to the world.

Like the Revolution, the Civil War reached its climax in Virginia. Replacing a succession of hapless Union commanders, Ulysses S. Grant in 1864–65 drove Lee's army to defeat. In the spring of 1865, the besieged city of Petersburg fell, Lee was forced to evacuate Richmond, and on April 9 the exhausted Army of Northern Virginia surrendered to Grant at Appomattox Court House. Virginia was at low ebb. A generation of young men had been decimated, a wealth of homes and farms had been destroyed, Richmond and Petersburg lay in ashes, railways and bridges had been demolished, and a way of life had gone with the wind. In his moving farewell to his troops, Lee said:

After four years of arduous service, marked by unsurpassed courage and fortitude, the Army of Northern Virginia has been compelled to yield to overwhelming numbers and resources. I need not tell the survivors of so many hard-fought battles, who have remained steadfast to the last, that I have consented to this result from no distrust of them; but feeling that valour and devotion could accomplish nothing that could compensate for the loss that would attend the continuation of this contest, I have determined to avoid the useless sacrifice of those whose past service has endeared them to their countrymen.

By the terms of the agreement, officers and men can return to their homes and remain there until exchanged. You will take with you the satisfaction that proceeds from the consciousness of duty faithfully performed; and I earnestly pray that a merciful God will extend to you His blessing and protection. With an increasing admiration of your constancy and devotion to your country and a grateful remembrance of your kind and generous consideration of myself, I bid you an affectionate farewell.

Men wept as they saddled up their horses, bade good-bye to tentmates, and started for farms and homes scattered across ruined Virginia. Just as the Old Dominion's call for union in 1776 had been the high point of her career, the desolation of Appomattox was the low. A century would elapse before she would regain her rightful place in the sisterhood of states. Perhaps never again would she exert the influence of her formative years.

The wounds of war were followed by the sores of Reconstruction. Virginia's federally imposed "restored" government, which had been set up under Unionist Governor Francis Pierpont by the Wheeling Convention in 1862, triumphantly moved after Lee's surrender from its wartime seat at Alexandria into the capitol at Richmond, so recently the office of Jefferson Davis.

Although President Andrew Johnson had proposed mild treatment of the ravaged South, Radical Republicans in Congress determined to treat the region as conquered territory. Accordingly, when the Pierpont government held elections for a new Virginia Assembly and congressmen in October 1865, the Radical Republicans refused to seat the men elected. Virginia became District I under the Reconstruction Act of 1867, with General John Schofield in command at Richmond.

In 1866, after Congress enacted the Fourteenth Amendment guaranteeing equal rights to blacks, most ex-Confederates were barred from voting. Government in Virginia temporarily fell into the hands of "scallywags" (native white Unionists), "carpetbaggers" (ex-northerners), and freed slaves. Even so, Reconstruction in Virginia was probably more orderly and less severe than in any other southern state.

The Radical Republicans' strongest effort to reshape Virginia was the so-called Underwood Constitutional Convention, which met in Richmond in 1868 to revise Virginia's laws. With Republican John C. Underwood presiding, the convention voted for adult male suffrage regardless of race, for an oath of Union loyalty from jurors and officeholders, and for the disfranchisement of former Confederates. Fortunately, the latter provision was stricken by President Grant and Congress. After the Virginia Assembly had ratified the Fourteenth and Fifteenth amend-

ments, a chastened Virginia was permitted to return in 1870 to her place in Congress. Military rule came to an end. Virginia had reentered the Union.

The Civil War had interrupted the growth of railroad building, but this was resumed after Appomattox. Virginia's espousal of canals had proved to be a mistake, especially after the Baltimore and Ohio Railroad in 1830 had tapped the rich Ohio Valley market with a line from Baltimore to Cincinnati. Soon railroads sprang up between Petersburg and Weldon, North Carolina, between Winchester and Harper's Ferry, between Richmond and Fredericksburg, and elsewhere in the state. After 1865, these lines merged into regional systems, giving rise to such centers as Roanoke, Newport News, Clifton Forge, and Buena Vista.

Bankrupted by war, Virginia struggled after 1870 to repay the forty-five million dollars in interest it owed on prewar bonds issued to build turnpikes, canals, and railroads. Conservatives, who returned to power with the state's readmission to the Union in 1870, voted to repay the debt in full. However, General Billy Mahone of Petersburg, now a railroad president, disagreed. Arguing that state funds were more urgently needed to build the public schools decreed by the Underwood Constitution, his "Readjusters" broke with the Conservatives and in 1879 gained control of the Assembly. Mahone himself—a liberal Populist standing against a Conservative old guard—was elected to the United States Senate in 1881, and his lieutenant, William Cameron of Petersburg, was elected governor a year later. The brief-lived Readjuster legislature reduced the state debt by more than half, and Mahone's followers were vindicated by the Supreme Court's validation of their act.

The Readjusters under Mahone did much to "break the power of wealth and established privilege" in Virginia before they were swept from power after 1883 by the reviving Conservatives. They repealed a Conservative poll tax on voters, raised taxes on corporations, increased support for schools, and established a college at Petersburg to train black teachers. But Mahone's reforms came too fast for most whites, who saw in his program a repudiation of the time-honored planter consensus that had ruled Virginia before the war.

It was inevitable that a return of normalcy should bring back to power the coalition of planters, lawyers, and courthouse officeholders that had governed Virginia before 1866. Add the fact that the Democrats' candidate in 1886 was the colorful Fitzhugh Lee, ex-Confederate and nephew of "Marse Robert," and the doom of Mahone and his Republican allies seems foregone. Indeed, so bitterly did Virginia remember Reconstruction that it was not to elect another Republican governor until 1970. As a result, Virginia government for eighty-four years was a one-party affair, directed by a genteel Democratic "Organization," operating through party officials in counties and cities. The system survived until the retirement of Senator Harry Flood Byrd, Sr., in 1965.

Despite vast change in the world, Virginia's character changed little after the Civil War. Lee and his Confederates were virtually worshiped. The old planter class—white, Anglo-Saxon, Protestant, and largely rural—continued its paternalistic reign. Blacks, though legally free, remained dependent on "old massa" for jobs, tenant houses, and help. Despite the birth of public schools in 1870 under the Reverend William Henry Ruffner of Rockbridge, county officials often dragged their feet in supporting education. The old paternalism survived, moderated perhaps by the broadening egalitarianism of Baptists, Methodists, and other denominations.

The chief change—small at first—was the mushrooming of cities. Freed by Lincoln's Emancipation Proclamation in 1863, thousands of illiterate blacks fled farms and swarmed to federal posts at Norfolk, Hampton, and Alexandria in search of a livelihood. "Freedmen's towns" grew up as ghettos around military posts. Aided at first by the United States Freedmen's Bureau, these ex-slaves turned to whites for one-dollar- and two-dollar-a-week jobs.

At Newport News, industrialist Collis P. Huntington in the 1880s hired hundreds of these uprooted blacks to build his C & O Railroad terminals and his Chesapeake Dry Dock and Construction Company—later the Newport News shipyard. Unable to find work at home, other blacks moved north. To teach illiterate blacks, training schools were set up. One of these, created by General Samuel Armstrong at Old Point, became Hampton Institute.

But the rise of the blacks alarmed many citizens, and a convention was called in Richmond in 1901 to revise the liberal Underwood Constitution of 1869. The document it produced in 1902 —not submitted to referendum, as earlier constitutions had been—gave Virginia the narrowest electorate in the nation. The spirit of Jim Crow was evident in the constitution's prohibitions against racial mixing in schools, public conveyances, and restaurants. Not until the advent of the New Deal in 1933 were such restrictions removed, most of them by decisions of the United States Supreme Court.

The pace of Virginia life remained slow for three centuries. It was the leisured pace of the oxcart, the horse-drawn surrey, the graceful white steamer which wafted passengers over Chesapeake Bay and along endless green rivers. Suddenly all this changed. With the influx of Henry Ford's Model T, remote farm families were put within reach of public schools, cities, and jobs. One-room rural schools were consolidated, and peninsulas separated by waterways were united. Roads and schools became the commonwealth's chief concerns. After World War II, the rising standard of living gave a strong impetus to higher education.

Clearly, wars and industry diluted Virginia's individualism after 1918, bringing its values and racial patterns more into harmony with those of the North. Yet the Old Dominion in the new age lost something precious in the decline of manners, the weakening of home and religious influences, and the rude quickening of life's pace. On the other hand, it gained in literacy, living standards, creature comforts, health, and that omnipotent new deity "public welfare."

In literature and the arts, Virginia continued to contribute modestly, aided by the patronage of cities and colleges. The romantic fictions of John Esten Cooke, Mary Johnston, James Branch Cabell, Amélie Rives Troubetzkoy and John Fox, Jr., gave way to the greater realism of Ellen Glasgow, William Styron, and Tom Wolfe. A surge of scholarship produced an eminent array of historians and biographers, including Douglas Freeman, Lenoir Chambers, David Mays, Dumas Malone, and Virginius Dabney, all of them winners of Pulitzer prizes.

In the graphic arts Virginia's role was less impressive. In the Civil War period, some Virginians achieved repute as painters. But agrarian Virginia had nothing to compare with the painting schools of Philadelphia, Boston, and the Hudson Valley.

Of memorable poets, playwrights, or musicians Virginia had few, except for composer John Powell of Richmond and—briefly—the now-famous English composer, Frederick Delius, who lived as a young man in twentieth-century Danville.

Blacks have had a growing role in recent Virginia. Besides Booker T. Washington and Robert Moton—both educated at Hampton Institute—they have produced hundreds of worthy clergy, teachers, musicians, and artisans. Thomas Nelson Page testified to the devotion of blacks and whites in the paternalistic society, now largely faded. Notable in recent Virginia have been black entertainers like Bill "Bojangles" Robinson of Richmond, Pearl Bailey and Ella Fitzgerald of Newport News, and singer Camilla Williams of Danville. The full flowering of black talent is yet to come, however.

Compared to the wealth of early leaders, recent Virginia seems unproductive. Except for Woodrow Wilson, born at Staunton in 1856, few twentieth-century Virginians have greatly influenced national affairs. Carter Glass of Lynchburg fathered the Federal Reserve System in 1913, and Harry Byrd, Sr., was a potent anti–New Dealer in the Senate from 1933 until 1965. Despite the state's strong judicial record, no Virginian was appointed to the United States Supreme Court from the outbreak of the Civil War until Lewis Powell, Jr., of Richmond was named to the court in 1971.

Virginia's extreme conservatism kept her out of the mainstream of national affairs from the Reconstruction until the 1970s, when national politics took a conservative turn after long years of liberal domination. As happened earlier in the industrial North, the Old Dominion has lost much of its peculiar political flavor—and some of its political gentility—since the New Deal. As capital accumulates in Virginia's cities and as industry comes south, gentlemanly consensus politics have given way to the polarization of capital and labor.

Even so, the high standards of honor that have marked most of Virginia's politics survive, together with a *noblesse oblige* that contrasts happily with the atmosphere in recent Maryland and New Jersey politics. Personal honor and political morality are jealously preserved in the home state of Washington, Jefferson, Madison, Lee, and Woodrow Wilson. May they always be so.

Two world wars have radically changed Virginia and the nation. The simple past is hopelessly remote.

The effect on Virginia of postwar events has been profound. Her population has surged upward from 2,677,773 in the census of 1940 to 4,456,349 in 1970. Particularly in those portions of the state that form part of the northeastern urban corridor—stretching from Boston south to Norfolk—cities, suburbs, and military bases unroll continuously. Heavy immigration from other states (Northern Neck Virginians call these immigrants "come-heres") has diluted traditional attitudes and accents. Virginia is no longer a "you-all" land.

Other change has come, too. The factory has supplanted the farm as the chief fount of Virginia's income, creating greater wealth but causing worse problems. Blacks are taking a larger part in community and school life—a revolution that has occurred with little violence but much anguish, especially in the "black belt" south of the James. Higher education has been brought within reach of nearly all by the state's creation of community colleges and by the expansion of older schools. Huge highway vans have taken over the carriage of most freight, to the detriment of railways and of the once-busy Chesapeake rivers and sea lanes.

The Virginian's attachment to hearth and history leads him to resist these changes, though to no effect. But at least he cherishes the old landmarks—St. Luke's Church, Stratford Hall, Fincastle—and celebrates such red-letter days as the landing at Jamestown (May 13), the victory at Yorktown (October 19), and the birthday of Lee (January 19). Indeed, no one is more dedicated than the Virginian to the preservation of his *lares* and *penates,* a movement begun by Anne Pamela Cunningham when she saved Mount Vernon for the public in 1852. The Association for the Preservation of Virginia Antiquities, begun in 1889, inspired other efforts. The largest, begun in 1926, was the restoration of Williamsburg by John D. Rockefeller, Jr.

Likewise, Virginia keeps the memory of great events of the past. She led in extensive Jamestown observances in 1907 and 1957, and she prompted the United States government to celebrate the culminating battle of the Revolution at Yorktown in 1881 and 1931. The two hundredth anniversary of the Revolution in 1976–81 again sees Virginia exerting national leadership, with ambitious plans unfolding at Yorktown, Alexandria, Charlottesville, and elsewhere.

An observant European has described Virginia as "the spoiled older sister of the States." Such indeed she may have been for many years—a commonwealth unduly conscious of her early primacy and unwilling to give in to a bland national average. But if this was indeed true, the twentieth century has forced the proud sister into the grudging semblance of conformity. At heart, however, Virginians are much as Governor Spotswood described them in 1716: "By their professions and actions, they seem to allow no jurisdiction, civil or ecclesiastical, but what is established by laws of their own making." Compare with this President Franklin Roosevelt's complaint against "too many Byrds in the Senate!"

Yes, Virginia in the 1970s is close in spirit to the Virginia of the 1670s: easygoing, friendly, old-fashioned, pleasure-loving, conventional, slow to rouse, moderate in religion, fond of privacy, respectful of precedent. Although no longer dominantly agricultural, her people have a profound love for the land—*their* land—that time and transplantation cannot erase.

This is the essence of Virginia—this and her pride in the character she has shown to the world. Washington, Jefferson, and Lee have become touchstones by which all else in Virginia must be measured. It is a worthy challenge for a people to live up to.

A Pictorial History

1

2

3

"Earth's only paradise," wrote the English poet Michael Drayton about Virginia, and it was indeed a beautiful land. On the Atlantic side of the Eastern Shore, Assateague Beach (1) attracted wildlife. Above the fall line, the land rose in ascending hills; a farm at Marion (2), in southwest Virginia, illustrates its contours. Some rivers flowed eastward to the coastal plain, while others, like the New River (3), drained westward. In the Valley of Virginia, the rich soil invited the planting of orchards (4). OVERLEAF: Valley farm at spring plowing time.

4

The Beautiful Land

Coastal Virginia was mild and flat, but hills and mountains appeared as settlers went westward. In Dismal Swamp, ancient cypress trees grew in turbid waters (1). In the Valley were rugged hills (2) that attracted Scotch-Irish and Germanic settlers in the eighteenth century. Across a creek near Lexington looms Natural Bridge (3), over which Indians and settlers were to pass. Not far away, on the present Blue Ridge Parkway, is Sharp Top (4); it supplied the Virginia stone for the Washington Monument.

4

1

Virginia's Indians

The Algonquian Indians who held Tidewater Virginia in 1607 were ruled by Chief Powhatan (1), depicted seated above his subjects in this detail from a map in Smith's *Generall Historie,* published in London in 1624. An Indian deer hunt showing characteristic Indian structures (2) is shown elsewhere in the *Historie,* as is a duck hunt (3). The richest pictorial record of the coastal Algonquians was painted by John White, leader of the Roanoke Island settlement in 1587. White's watercolor of a religious seer, "The Flyer" (4), was reproduced as an engraving in Theodore DeBry's *Virginia,* as was another of a chief's wife and child (5). A deerskin cloak (6), long identified as Powhatan's, was brought back to England and is now exhibited at the Ashmolean Museum at Oxford University. In 1645, Wenceslaus Hollar produced this portrait (7) of "An American of Virginia, Age 23," showing a chief wearing shells.

2

3

4

5

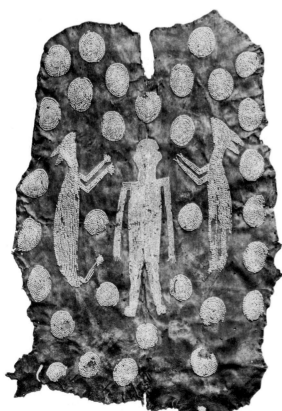

6

7

27

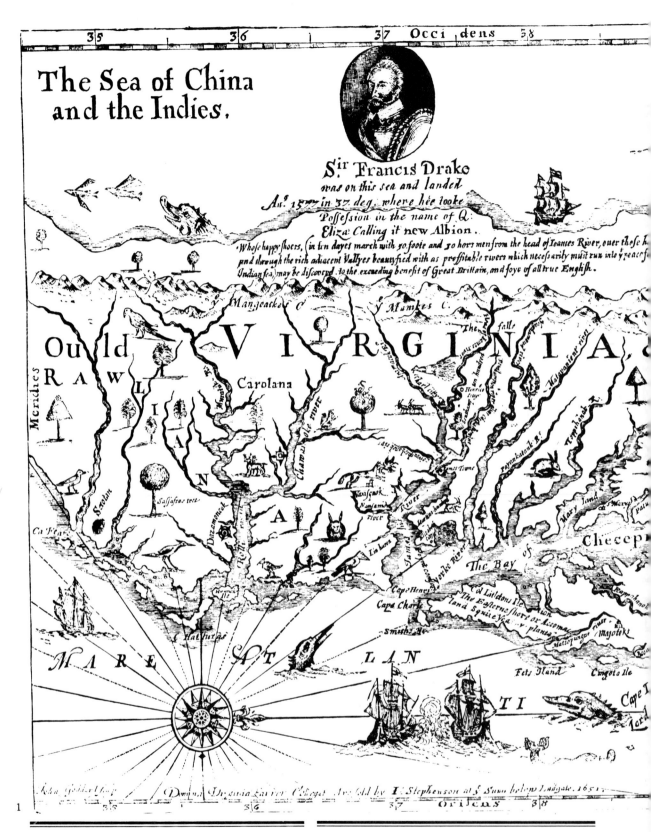

North America, or "Virginia," as the English first called it, was of unknown size and shape for years after the 1607 settlement. A map (1) published in England in 1651, showed Virginia as close to California, which Sir Francis Drake had touched in 1577. Virginia was named for Queen Elizabeth (2), "the Virgin Queen," by Sir Walter Raleigh (3), who in 1584 sent explorers there and the next year tried to plant a colony at Roanoke Island. Many books were printed in England about the new colony of Virginia, like *Nova Britannia* (4), issued in 1609.

2 3

4

1

3

2

4

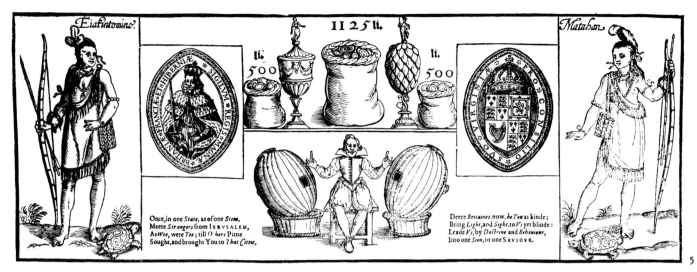

Although named for Queen Elizabeth, Virginia was not permanently settled until 1607—four years after the queen died. The title page of John Smith's *Generall Historie* bears likenesses of Elizabeth, her successor, King James I, and his son, Prince Charles (1). The early arms of the colony (2) bore a Latin motto meaning "Behold, Virginia gives the fifth kingdom." The other kingdoms which the king of England claimed were England and Wales considered as one, France, Scotland, and Ireland. The first settlers sailed into Chesapeake Bay through two capes, naming one Cape Henry (3), for King James's eldest son, and the other Cape Charles, for his second. Sir Thomas Smythe (4), a wealthy merchant, headed the Virginia Company. A lottery was advertised for the benefit of the company in 1615. Some prizes and Indians are shown in the broadside announcing it (5). Another broadside (6), published to lure settlers, lists Virginia's products.

A valuation of the Commodities growing and to be had in *Virginia:* valued in the year, 1621.

And since those Times improved in all more or lesse, in some ⅓, in others ¼, in many double, and in some treble.

Iron, ten pounds the Tun.
Silke Coddes, two shillings six pence the pound.
   Raw silk, 13s.4d. the pound, now at 25s. and 28. *per* pound.
   Silke grasse to be used for Cordage, 6d. the pound : but we hope it will serve for many better uses, and so yeeld a far greater rate, wherof there can never be too much planted. Of this Q. *Elizabeth* had a silke Gowne made.
   Hemp, from 10s. to 22s. the hundred,
   Flax, from 22s, to 30s. the hundred.
   Cordage, from 20s. to 24s. the hundred.
   Cotton wooll, 8d. the pound.
   Hard pitch, 5s. the hundred.
   Tarre, 5s. the hundred.
   Turpentine, 12s. the hundred.
   Rozen, 5s. the hundred.
   Maddet crop, 4○ s. the hundred : course madder, 25s. the hundred.
   Woad, from 12s. to 20 the hundred.
   Annice seeds, 40s. the hundred.
   Powder Sugar, Panels, Muscavadoes and whites, 25s. 40. and 3l. the hundred.　　　H 3　　　Sturgeon, 6

The Adventures of John Smith

1

2

The father figure at early Jamestown was John Smith (1), who led the settlers in the colony's first few years. Injured in the winter of 1609, he returned to England but continued to promote Virginia in his writings. He claimed that the Indian princess Pocahontas (2) had interceded with her father, Chief Powhatan, to save him from execution. Pocahontas never married the bachelor Smith but wed John Rolfe, who introduced Spanish-type tobacco at Jamestown and launched a profitable trade. In his *Generall Historie of Virginia, New-England, and the Summer Isles,* Smith told of his adventures from 1607 to 1609 among the Algonquians. Some of these adventures are shown in an illustration from the book (3). At upper left, Indian bowmen celebrate his capture. At upper center, Powhatan is shown enthroned; Smith is seated among priests and conjurers. At lower right is a depiction of Smith's rescue from Powhatan's headsman by Pocahontas. At bottom center is Smith's map of Virginia's coast south from Cape Henry, part of which was later to be included in North Carolina. The lower left panel shows Smith's capture by the Indians after a battle in 1607 and his subjugation of the chief of the Paspaheghs two years later.

3

Life in Jamestown

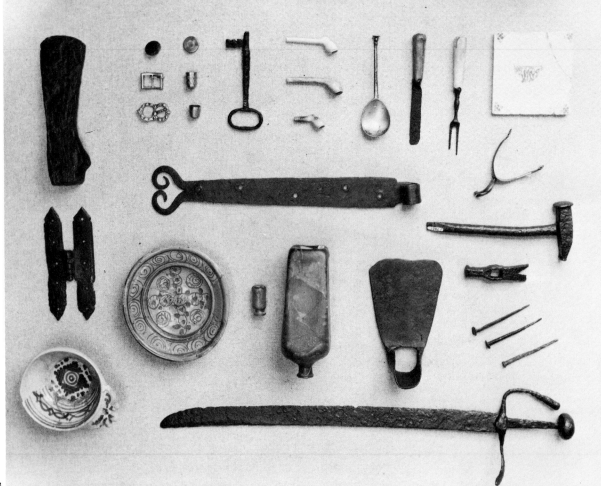

Excavations have unearthed fragments of many crude seventeenth-century objects dating from the ninety-two year period when Jamestown served as Virginia's capital. A plaster mask (1), believed to have been part of a mantel or wall decoration, was found at one site. Foundations (2) of the first state-house facing the James River were excavated by the National Park Service in the 1930s. A variety of household items (3) have been unearthed from Jamestown's middens and basements, including ax and adze heads, slipware pottery, buckles, buttons, keys, Dutch gin bottles, clay pipes, kitchen utensils, flatware, and hardware. Pottery was first brought from England and, after a few decades, made in Virginia. The various utensils shown here (4) are slipware, decorated with sgraffito designs. From some long-gone mantel, a Delftware tile (5) was dug up—one of many showing sports of John Smith's day. Thousands of artifacts like these are preserved and exhibited in the Jamestown Visitor Center of the Colonial National Historical Park.

35

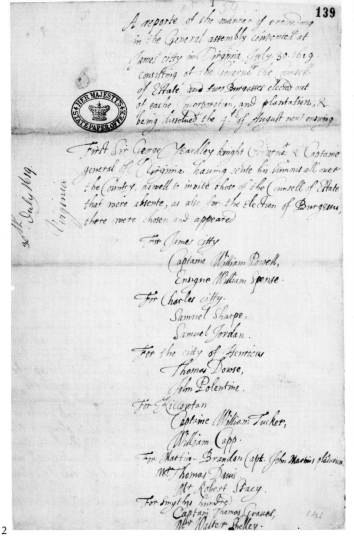

1

A reporte of the manner of proceeding
in the General assembly conuented at
James citty in Virginia July. 30. 1619
consisting of the Gouernor the counsell
of Estate and two Burgesses elected out
of eache incorporation, and plantation; &
being dissolued the 4th of August next ensuing.

First Sir George Yeardley knight Gouernor & Captayne
generall of Virginia. hauing sente his summons all over
the Country, aswell to inuite those of the Counsell of Estate
that were absente, as also for the election of Burgesses
there were chosen and appeared.

    For James citty
        Captaine William Powell,
        Ensigne William Spense.
    For Charles citty.
        Samuel Sharpe,
        Samuel Jordan.
    For the citty of Henricus
        Thomas Dowse,
        John Polentine.
    For Kiccowtan
        Captaine William Tucker,
        William Capp.
    For Martin-Brandon Capt. John Martins plantation
        Mr. Thomas Davis
        Mr. Robert Stacy.
    For Smythes hundred
        Captain Thomas Graves,
        Mr. Walter Shelley.

2

3

36

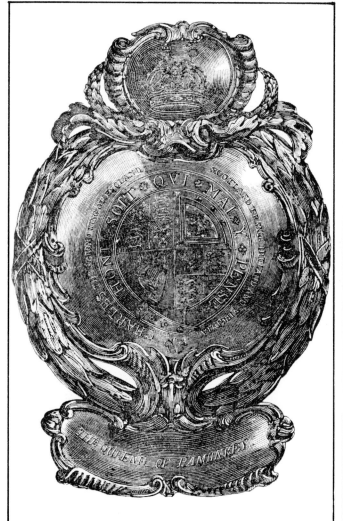

5

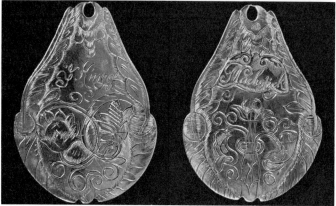

6

In 1618 Sir Edwin Sandys (1) succeeded Sir Thomas Smythe as head of the Virginia Company. He introduced the beginning of self-rule in Virginia, approving a "Great Charter of Privileges, Orders, and Laws" and authorizing an annual Assembly, vaguely analogous to the House of Commons. The first Assembly met at Jamestown in 1619, and its record (2) was sent to London by John Pory, its clerk. To replace the harsh regime of Deputy Governor Sir Thomas Dale (3), the company sent over Governor Sir George Yeardley. After several Indian massacres which killed many colonists, efforts were made to attain peace with the Indians; medals made of silver were given after a peace treaty at Middle Plantation (later Williamsburg) in 1677 to the queen of the Pamunkeys (4), the king of the Potomacs (5), and the king of the Machodocs (6). One of the many early broadsides that described progress in the often embattled colony was *The New Life of Virginea* (7), printed in London in 1617.

THE
NEW LIFE
of Virginea :
DECLARING THE
FORMER SVCCESSE AND PRE-
sent estate of that plantation, being the second
part of *Noua Britannia*.

Published by the authoritie of his Maiesties
Counsell of *Virginea*.

LONDON,
Imprinted by *Felix Kyngston* for *William Welby*, dwelling at the
signe of the Swan in Pauls Churchyard. 1 6 1 2.

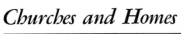

Churches and Homes

1

2

3

The first buildings of early Virginia were of wood, but brick soon came into use for some churches and planters' houses. Bacon's Castle (1) was built in Surry County about 1655 by planter Arthur Allen. Its gabled ends and Jacobean chimneys hark back to English styles. Near Norfolk, a former indentured servant, Adam Thoroughgood, began about 1634 to build his house (2). A few years later, settlers south of the James began to erect the church, later known as St. Luke's Church (3), Smithfield. The reconstructed arched rear window (4) and the brick tower (5) are from Jamestown Church.

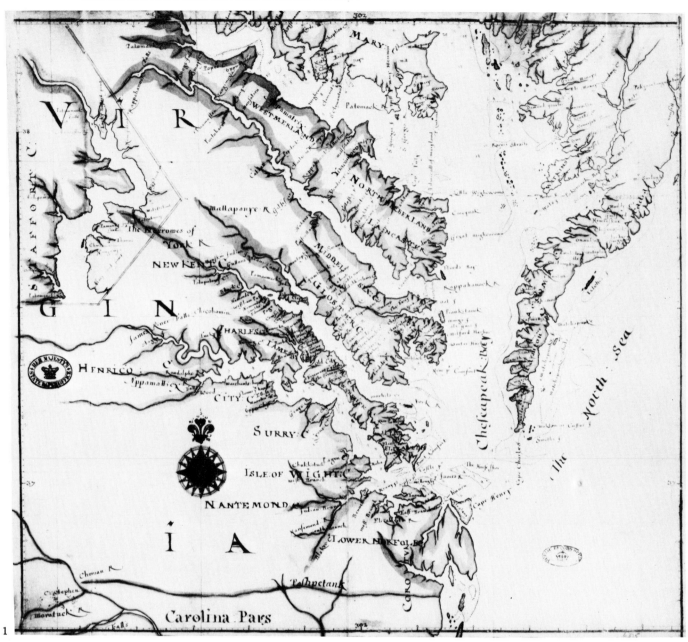

1

2

Tobacco became Virginia's gold in 1612 and remained so for two hundred years. By the time this map (1) was made, most of Tidewater's river frontage was divided into plantations and farms. "Virginia tobacco" became a staple of Britain's expanding imperial trade, cited in the labels of British tobacconists of the seventeenth and eighteenth centuries (2, 3, 4). The choicest Virginia tobacco of all—fine-leafed and sweet-scented—was grown along the York River, glamorously depicted in this label (5) showing a planter receiving rolled hogsheads ready for shipment to Britain.

BROMLEYS
best Virginia,
Friday Street

Boxes, Chests, and
Packing Cases made & Sold

Hulleys Best Virgin?
at ÿ Black Boy & Tobac?
Rolc in off dlle in York
Buildings in ÿ Strand

The settlers lived a precarious life. In 1622 the Indians massacred 347 of them (1), reducing the young colony's population by one-fourth. Virginia's coat of arms (2), seen at left, was displayed by the colony's governors. Most memorable of the seventeenth-century governors was Sir William Berkeley (3), who served during most of the years from 1645 to 1677, attracting during the Cromwellian period a number of well-to-do royalist emigrés who strengthened Virginia's Cavalier character. He was recalled to England after the Virginia rebellion led by Nathaniel Bacon in 1676. Among other seventeenth-century leaders were William Randolph (4) of Henrico County; Matthew Page (5) of Gloucester; and Reverend James Blair (6) of Williamsburg. Blair, a Scotsman, came to Virginia as an Anglican missionary and founded the College of William and Mary in 1693, serving as its president until his death fifty years later.

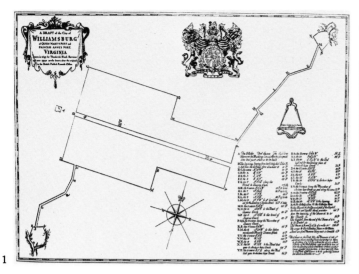

3

A new capital, Williamsburg, was created in 1699 at Middle Plantation, midway between the James and the York (1). Francis Louis Michel sketched the first brick church (2) of Bruton Parish in 1702 and the first structure of the College of William and Mary (3), burned in 1705 and replaced by 1718 in a slightly different form. An unknown artist depicted Williamsburg's principal buildings (4) about 1744. The new capital grew handsomely during the governorship of Alexander Spotswood (5) from 1710 to 1722. Other influential governors were Francis Fauquier (6) (the picture, long thought to be of him, may show his son); and Lord Botetourt (7), whose statue was erected at the Capitol after his death in 1770.

4

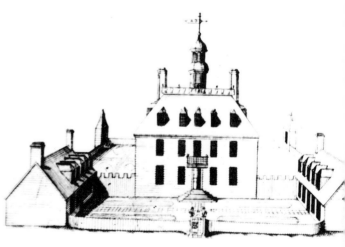

5

6

7

At Williamsburg, the handsome new brick Capitol (1) was built in 1704 at the east end of the mile-long Duke of Gloucester Street. Roughly midway between the Capitol and the College of William and Mary, the colony's Powder Magazine (2) was erected in 1715. About 1720, the Assembly grudgingly appropriated the last sums needed for the Governor's Palace (3), handsomely placed at the head of a greensward intersecting Duke of Gloucester Street. As the seat of His Majesty's viceroy in the largest British colony in the New World, the palace was a showplace. Its wrought-iron entrance bore a gilded crown, faced by lion and unicorn (4). The palace ballroom and supper room beyond (5) were added to the rear of the building about 1751, opening onto beautiful, formal gardens. Here the governor entertained colonials and visiting officials.

PAGES 48–49. The two houses of Virginia's Assembly met in the Capitol. The chamber of the House of Burgesses is shown on page 48; on page 49 is the Council chamber.

3

4

5

1

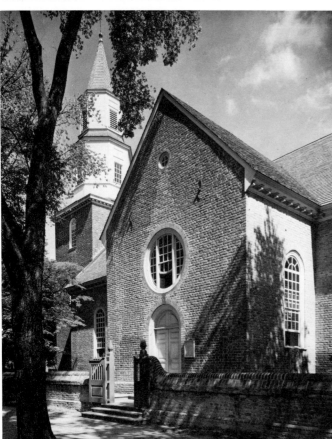

3

2

5

By PERMISSION of the Honble *ROBERT DINWIDDIE*, Efq; His Majefty's Lieutenant-Governor, and Commander in Chief of the Colony and Dominion of *Virginia*.

By a Company of COMEDIANS, *from* LONDON, *At the* THEATRE *in* WILLIAMSBURG, On *Friday* next, being the 15th of *September*, will be prefented, A PLAY, Call'd,

THE MERCHANT of *VENICE*.

(Written by *Shakefpear*.)
The Part of *ANTONIO* (the MERCHANT) to be perform'd by
Mr. CLARKSON.
GRATIANO, by Mr. SINGLETON,
Lorenzo, (with Songs in Character) by Mr. ADCOCK.
The Part of *BASSANIO* to be perform'd by
Mr. RIGBY.
Duke, by Mr. Wynell.
Salanio, by Mr. Herbert.
The Part of *LAUNCELOT*, by Mr. HALLAM.
And the Part of *SHYLOCK*, (the JEW) to be perform'd by
Mr. MALONE.
The Part of *NERISSA*, by Mrs. ADCOCK,
Jeffica, by Mrs. Rigby.
And the Part of *PORTIA*, to be perform'd by
Mrs. HALLAM.
With a new occafional PROLOGUE.
To which will be added, a FARCE, call'd,
The ANATOMIST: OR, SHAM DOCTOR.
The Part of *Monfieur le Medecin*, by
Mr. RIGBY.
And the Part of *BEATRICE*, by Mrs. ADCOCK.
*** No Perfon, whatfoever, to be admitted behind the Scenes.
BOXES. 7s. 6d. PIT and BALCONIES, 5s. 9d. GALLERY, 3s. 9d.
To begin at Six o'Clock.

Vivat Rex.

THE Snow *Frances*, Paul Loyall, Mafter, who will be at his Moorings, at Capt. *Danfie's*, in *Pamunky*, will take in Tobacco for *London*, either from *York* or *Rappahanock* River, at 7 *l. per* Ton, with Liberty of Confignment. Gentlemen inclined to fhip, are defired to fend their Orders to Mr. *John Norton*, Mr. *Hugh Miller*, the Mafter on Board, the Printer hereof, or to

Robert Tucker.

N. B. She is a fine new Veffel, and completely fitted.

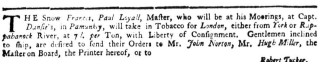

Completed in 1697, the College of William and Mary attracted the capital of the colony to its site at Middle Plantation within three years. After the original college burned in 1705, it was rebuilt (1). William and Mary served as a preparatory school, a college, and an Anglican seminary. Expanding, Williamsburg required a larger church; to serve its needs, Bruton Parish Church (2) was completed in 1715. In its governor's pew, at left (3), a succession of notables worshipped. Williamsburg's public gaol (4) held at various times the henchmen of Blackbeard and the revolutionary military captive Colonel Henry Hamilton. A favorite actress in Williamsburg was Nancy Hallam (5), here seen in *Cymbeline*. A visiting company's playbill (6) lists plays and performers at the Williamsburg theater, the first in the thirteen colonies.

1

2

An Age of Luxury

To be SOLD, by the Subscriber, near the Capitol, *in* Williamsburg,

GENUINE *French* Claret, at 40 *s. per* Dozen, Samples whereof may be had at 4 *s.* a Bottle, net *Barbadoes* Rum at 5 *s. per* Gallon; alſo fine *Madeira* Wine, *Engliſh* Beer, and *Hughes's* Cyder, at the common Rates; alſo a Caſk of fine Hogs-Lard, of about 230 *lb.* Weight, with ſeveral Pots of Capers and Anchovies.

2   *Daniel Fiſher.*

Britain's world trade in the eighteenth century brought wealth to many tobacco planters. They built handsome Georgian houses along Tidewater rivers, and imported furniture and luxurious clothes from England. Along the James in about 1740, the Hill family built Shirley, (1), still home to the descendants of the Hills and the Carters. At Carter's Grove (2), built in the 1750s on the James near Williamsburg, the panelled hall contained a stairway so wide that British raider Banastre Tarleton was said to have ridden his horse up it during the Revolution. At Fredericksburg, Fielding Lewis in 1752–56 built Kenmore (3, 4) on his 861 acre estate for his second wife, Betty Washington, sister of George. In the affluent pre-Revolutionary years, merchants advertised in Williamsburg's *Virginia Gazette* (5). Horse-racing spread with the importation from England of thoroughbreds like Shark (6), bought in 1786 by Benjamin Hyde of Fredericksburg, after a stellar English career.

Living like the English country gentry of Fielding's *Tom Jones*, planters adopted many customs of rural England. Fox hunting became popular in the mid-eighteenth century. *The End of the Hunt* shows sportsmen clearing a rail fence in upland Virginia.

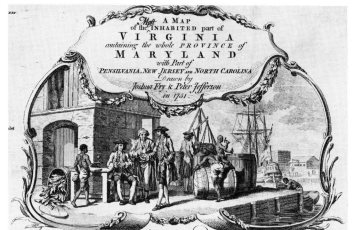

1

2

3

Plantation life was year-round work. In the fall, hogsheads of tobacco were shipped, as shown in the cartouche of the Fry-Jefferson map of Virginia in 1751 (1). An English tobacco label (2) shows blacks working for a planter. A page from a planter's ledger (3) shows his expenses. An important pre-Revolutionary port was Yorktown (4), on the York, with homes of the Nelsons and Amblers fronting the river. One hazard of shipping was piracy, as practiced by Edward Teach, alias Blackbeard (5), who was defeated by Governor Spotswood's ships in 1718 and beheaded. Tobacco warehouse receipts (6) were used for money, as Britain's colonies were short of currency. Slaves were imported and bred to work tobacco, but they frequently fled. Advertisements for fugitives were common, like this one in Williamsburg's *Virginia Gazette* (7).

5

James River,
No. 271

Thomas Warehouse, the *30th* — Day of *July*, 1743

THIS shall oblige us, the Subscribers, our, and each of our Executors and Administrators, to pay, upon Demand, to *Saml Allen* or his Order, at the above-mentioned Warehouse, *five hundred sixty one* Pounds of good merchantable *Arro* Tobacco, according to the Directions of the Act of Assembly, *For amending the Staple of Tobacco, and preventing Frauds in His Majesty's Customs*; it being for the like Quantity received. Witness our Hands,

561

Robt. Burton
Cleab. Cocke

6

March 10, 1752.

RAN away from the Subscriber, living in *Prince George* County, about a Fortnight ago, a lusty well-set *Virginia*-born Negroe Man Slave, named *Harry*; he is a smooth-tongued cunning Fellow, and it's probable will endeavour to impose on People, by pretending to be what he is not; and it's not unlikely will change his Name; he is between 30 and 40 Years of Age, about 5 Feet 10 Inches high, and had on when he went away, an Oznabrigs Shirt, a Cotton Waistcoat and Breeches, or a Yellow, and a Pair of Breeches not dy'd. Whoever will take up and secure him, so that I may have him again, shall have Two Pistoles if taken up on the South Side of *James* River, if in *Carolina*, or the North Side of *James* River, Three Pistoles Reward, besides what the Law allows, paid by

William Broadnax.

7

Wealthy planter dynasties were numerous in lower Virginia before the Revolution. Among the leaders—all influential—were Robert "King" Carter (1) of Lancaster County; Thomas Lee (2) of Westmoreland; Daniel Parke II (3) of York; and William Byrd II (4) of Charles City. Byrd was the Virginia leader of an expedition to project the colony's southern dividing line with North Carolina in 1738. A map (5) whose drawing he supervised survives, along with his diaries, journals, and other writings. Two of the handsomest of the great houses constructed by the planters were Stratford Hall (6), built by Thomas Lee in Westmoreland about 1727, and Westover (7), built by William Byrd II in Charles City about 1730. Descendants of the great planters preserved their family holdings after the colonial period, in many cases intermarrying and creating a highly regarded planter aristocracy.

Into the Uplands

Eastern Virginians pioneered the settlement of the uplands; they were soon joined by Scotch-Irish and German immigrants. Dr. Thomas Walker (1) of Albemarle explored the western mountains and found Cumberland Gap in 1750. On the Great Wagon Road through the Valley, William Ingles operated a ferry and tavern (2) after 1762 at New River, near the present Radford. The Kilgore family built a fort house (3) about 1785 close to the beginning of the Wilderness Road through Cumberland Gap. At Waterford, in northern Virginia, Quaker Amos Janney built a mill (4) about 1755 to grind wheat and corn. Another fort house, Fort Egypt (5), near Luray, was constructed on a stone foundation, like the old log house at Waterford (6), shown above. At right (7) is another early Waterford dwelling.

Cumberland Gap

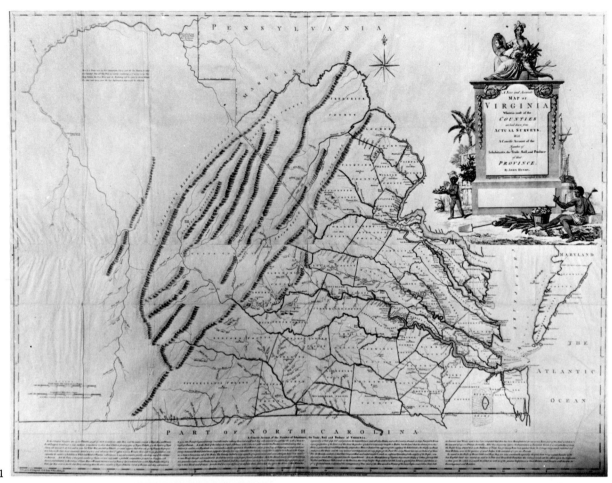

1

2

3

Virginia's "land hunger" was clear from the first. It led to early westward exploration and trade with the Indians. By the year 1770, when John Henry's "New and Accurate Map of Virginia" (1) was published in London, settlement was ready to leap the forbidding Appalachians into the Ohio River valley. Daniel Boone (2), a backwoodsman living in North Carolina, led several groups into the Kentucky territory before the Revolution, and in 1775 he cleared a narrow "Wilderness Road" through the gap in the Cumberland Mountains (3) which Thomas Walker had discovered in 1750. Through it, pioneers went on foot into Kentucky, many to be slaughtered by Indians on that "Dark and Bloody Ground." The gap lies today near the juncture (4) of Virginia, Kentucky, North Carolina, and West Virginia.

4

1

2

An ACADEMY.

PRINCE EDWARD, *Sept.* 1, 1775.

BY the generous Exertions of several Gentlemen in this and some of the neighbouring Counties, very large Contributions have lately been made for erecting and supporting a public ACADEMY near the Courthouse in this County. Their Zeal for the Interests of Learning and Virtue has met with such Success, that they were enabled to let the Buildings in *March* last to several Undertakers, who are proceeding in their Work with the greatest Expedition. A very valuable Library of the best Writers, both ancient and modern, on most Parts of Science and polite Literature, is already procured; with Part of an Apparatus to facilitate the Studies of the Mathematicks and Natural Philosophy, which we expect in a short Time to render complete.—The Academy will certainly be opened on the 10th of next *November*: It is to be distinguished by the Name of HAMPDEN-SIDNEY, and will be subject to the Visitation of twelve Gentlemen of Character and Influence in their respective Counties; the immediate and acting Members being chiefly of the Church of *England*. The Number of Visitors and Trustees will probably be increased as soon as the Distractions of the Times shall so far cease as to enable its Patrons to enlarge its Foundations.——The Students will all board and study under the same Roof, provided for by a common Steward, except such as choose to take their Boarding in the Country. The Rates, at the utmost, will not exceed 10l. Currency *per Annum* to the Steward, and 4l. Tuition Money; 20s. of this being always paid at Entrance.

The System of Education will resemble that which is adopted in the College of *New Jersey*; save, that a more particular Attention shall be paid to the Cultivation of the *English* Language than is usually done in Places of public Education. Three Masters and Professors are ready to enter in *November*, and as many more may be easily procured as the increased Number of Students may at any Time hereafter require. And our Prospects at present are so extremely flattering that it is probable we shall be obliged to procure two Professors more before the Expiration of the Year. The Public may rest assured that the Whole shall be conducted on the most *catholic* Plan. Parents, of every Denomination, may be at full Liberty to require their Children to attend on any Mode of Worship which either Custom or Conscience has rendered most agreeable to them. For our Fidelity, in every Respect, we are cheerfully willing to pledge our Reputation to the Public; which may be the more relied on, because our whole Success depends upon their favourable Opinion. Our Character and Interest, therefore, being both at Stake, furnish a strong Security for our avoiding all Party Instigations; for our Care to form good men, and good Citizens, on the common and universal Principles of Morality, distinguished from the narrow Tenets which form the Complexion of any Sect; and for our Assiduity in the whole Circle of Education.

SAMUEL S. SMITH.

P. S. The principal Building of the Academy not being yet completed, those Gentlemen who desire their Children to enter immediately will be obliged to take Lodgings for them in the Neighbourhood, during the Winter Season; which may be done in Houses sufficiently convenient, on very reasonable Terms. 4

3

The Scotch-Irish immigrants and their ministers in 1749 created the first school in the Valley of Virginia. By 1780 they had moved their Presbyterian "log college" to Lexington (1), naming it Liberty Hall and installing Rev. William Graham (2) as master. In 1775 Presbyterians of Prince Edward County announced in the *Virginia Gazette* (3) the creation of an academy, which opened the next year as Hampden-Sydney College. Its first president was Reverend Samuel Stanhope Smith (4), a graduate of the College of New Jersey, which was later to be known as Princeton. On the frontier at Draper's Meadows, later Blacksburg, Colonel William Preston built his Smithfield plantation (5) before the Revolution. An early upland hostelry was Michie's Tavern (6), which was subsequently moved to Charlottesville. It served travelers who traversed pioneer Albemarle County, when roads were few. Such taverns provided food, beds, and strong drink for weary travelers.

4

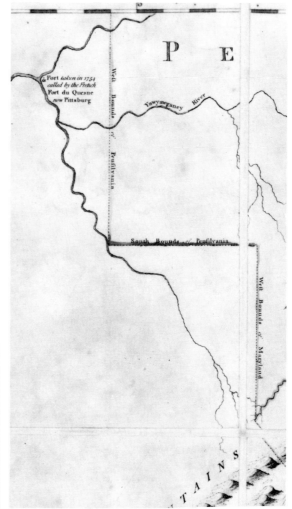

4

5

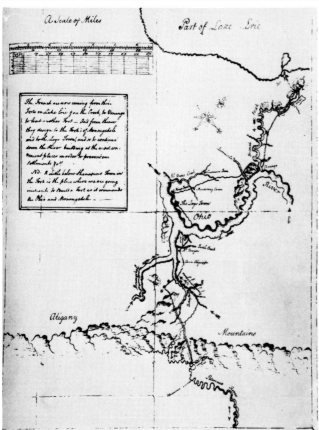

6

Because of the crown's grant of western Virginia lands to the Fairfaxes, a young Virginia surveyor, George Washington, grew familiar with the land and was able to lead war parties there. He was sent as a militia officer (1) to the frontier in the French and Indian Wars. Fauquier and Culpeper counties (2), in which young Washington spent much of his youth, are shown in a detail from John Henry's map of 1770. A reconstructed brick house (3), representing Washington's birthplace, stands at Wakefield in Westmoreland County. The field desk (4) that Washington carried on his travels still survives. Young Washington led an important mission against French troops at Fort Duquesne, near the present Pittsburgh, shown in another map detail (5). Washington's surveying skills helped him make maps, like this one (6) of his first mission against the French near Lake Erie in 1754. These experiences later led to his selection as commander in chief of the American army during the Revolution.

1

2

The Plantation Aristocracy

Many people worked hard on plantations to make leisure for a few. Frances Parke Custis (1) grew up on the estate of her father, Colonel John Custis IV, at Williamsburg. In 1725, at age fourteen, she was limned by an itinerant painter. Elizabeth Jaquelin (2) was painted at her family's Jamestown plantation in 1722. A folk painting resembling Mount Vernon's landward aspect (3) showed the age's taste for classical balance in its layout of dependencies, overseer's house, and servants' quarters. Ships calling in Virginia were often careened and overhauled at Gosport—now Portsmouth—as seen in a print (4) which shows H.M.S. *Thetis Bay* upended. Ship sailings were advertised in advance, as in this example from the *Pennsylvania Gazette* for October 27, 1747 (5). During years when Britain was at war with France or other Continental powers, tobacco ships formed into a convoy in lower Chesapeake Bay each fall and spring to permit protection by royal naval ships at sea.

Philadelphia, October 27. 1748.
For St. CHRISTOPHERS,
The BRIGANTINE
JANE,
ISAAC HARDTMAN
Commander :
Now lying at Samuel M' Call junior's wharff : For freight or paſſage agree with Joſeph Sims, or ſaid maſter on board.

Philadelphia, October 27. 1748.
For *Potomack* River, in *Virginia*, in three Weeks,
The SNOW
DILIGENCE,
Thomas Francis
Commander ;
Now lying at Carpenter's wharff. Any perſon that has any goods to ſhip on board her, may apply to the Maſter, at his lodgings, at Mr. Jonathan Evans's, in Front-ſtreet, or on board the ſnow.

1

WILLIAMSBURG, *September* 24, 1773.

TH^e publick Hospital established by an Act
of the General Assembly for the Reception of Ideots, Lunaticks,
and other Persons of unsound Minds, being now completed, Notice is
hereby given that the Court of Directors will meet at the said Hospital,
on Tuesday the 12th of October next, to receive all such Persons as may
be sent thereto according to the Directions of the said Act, and that at the
Court, for the same Purpose, and the better ordering the general Business
of the Hospital, will meet on the same Day in every succeeding Week,
till further Notice.

It is hoped that the Magistrates in the several Counties will in every
Instance distinguish between such Persons as have no Estates and those
who are able to defray the Whole or Part of the Expense of their Support and Maintenance as the Law requires, and that none but such as
are proper Objects of the Act of Assembly will be sent to the said Hospital.

By Order of the Court of Directors.   (4)   JACOB BRUCE, Clerk.

2

3

4

5

6

Virginia was the first colony to open a "lunatick asylum," or mental hospital. Started in 1773 at Williamsburg (1), it was the first unit in what was eventually a statewide system of mental hospitals. The *Virginia Gazette* in 1773 in Williamsburg welcomed "Ideots, Lunaticks, and other Persons of unsound Minds" to the asylum (2). The first professor of medicine in Virginia was Dr. James McClurg (3), who in 1779 taught briefly at the College of William and Mary. Another important doctor, Ephraim McDowell of Rockbridge County (4), performed a pioneering operation: removal of an ovarian tumor. At Fredericksburg, Hugh Mercer operated an apothecary shop (5), still preserved for visitors. Household remedies were advertised by William Pasteur of Williamsburg (6) in an advertisement in the *Virginia Gazette.* Sufferers from "rheumatism," as arthritic complaints were then called, often took the warm baths at Bath County's Warm Springs (7).

The Revolution Begins

SEPTEMBER 8, 1775.   THE   NUMBER 32

VIRGINIA   GAZETTE.

ALWAYS FOR LIBERTY,   AND THE PUBLICK GOOD.

ALEXANDER PURDIE, PRINTER.

Patrick Henry (1) was an unsurpassed spokesman for colonial rights. His "Give me liberty or give me death" speech on March 23, 1775, spread across the Atlantic. Henry spoke in Richmond at the Virginia Convention at Henrico Parish Church (2) which later was to gain a steeple and the name St. John's. Then a resident of Hanover, the eloquent lawyer later moved to Charlotte County, in southern Virginia, where he practiced law in his Red Hill plantation office (3). After 1775, Williamsburg had two *Virginia Gazettes* when the Scotsman Alexander Purdie founded this pro-patriot sheet (4) in opposition to the existing loyalist *Gazette*. Virginia's harsh treatment in 1775 of loyalist merchants who traded with England was flayed in a cartoon (5) published that year in London. Shown on the gallows are the tar and feathers awaiting objectors to the nonimportation agreement. A few loyalists left Virginia, but most Virginians adhered to the patriot cause.

A CURE FOR THE REFRACT...

TOURT

TOBACCO.
A PRESENT
For
JOHN WILKES
Esq.
LORD MAYOR OF
LONDON.

Non Importation

The Resolves of
the county...

LIBERTY

1

2

3

4

5

6

7

8

Lord Dunmore (1), the last royal governor of Virginia, fled Williamsburg in 1775. Among his adversaries were George Mason (2) of Fairfax County, who wrote the Fairfax Resolves and the Declaration of Rights adopted by Virginia in 1776; Thomas Jefferson (3); and Edmund Randolph (4), who served on Washington's staff and in his first cabinet after the nation was formed. Many of their revolutionary ideas were developed in the Apollo Room (5) of Williamsburg's Raleigh Tavern. The published record of Virginia's 1776 convention contains the Declaration of Rights (6) and other epic documents. Nearly all Virginia's planters favored the Revolution, though many English and Scottish merchants opposed it and left the colony. Virginia issued its own money (7) after 1775. Wealthy Virginia revolutionary leaders risked much. George Mason's Gunston Hall (8) in Fairfax was typical of their great plantations.

Jefferson penned the Declaration of Independence after John Adams argued that "a Virginian should be at the head of this business." The document was signed July 4, 1776 (1), at the Pennsylvania statehouse, later called Independence Hall. In Williamsburg, printer Alexander Purdie

ARTICLES

OF

Confederation

AND

Perpetual Union

BETWEEN THE

STATES

OF

New Hampshire, Massachusetts Bay, Rhode Island, and Providence Plantations,
Connecticut, New York, New Jersey, Pennsylvania, Delaware, Maryland,
Virginia, North Carolina, South Carolina, and Georgia.

WILLIAMSBURG:
Printed by ALEXANDER PURDIE.

2

3

printed the Articles of Confederation (2), adopted by the colonies. George Washington's quiet leadership was recognized by the Conti-nental Congress in his selection as commander in chief. This miniature (3) is one of the earliest portraits painted of the new general.

1

2

3

As the most populous of the thirteen colonies, Virginia sent many soldiers to the Revolution. One of the most unusual was the Reverend John Peter Muhlenberg of Woodstock (1), who gave up his pulpit in 1776 and rose to be a general. Leader of a secret Virginia mission which defeated the British along the Ohio River and held the Northwest Territory for Virginia was George Rogers Clark (2). Peter Francisco (3) reputedly held off nine of Tarleton's British cavalrymen at Amelia in 1781. Daniel Morgan of Winchester (4) was one of Washington's ablest generals, winning at Saratoga and Cowpens. The tiny capital of Richmond (5) was attacked by renegade General Benedict Arnold and his British army on January 5, 1781; they burned buildings and took vital supplies. Hessian soldiers taken prisoner were encamped at Charlottesville (6) and Winchester. Many remained in Virginia after the war as farmers and artisans.

4

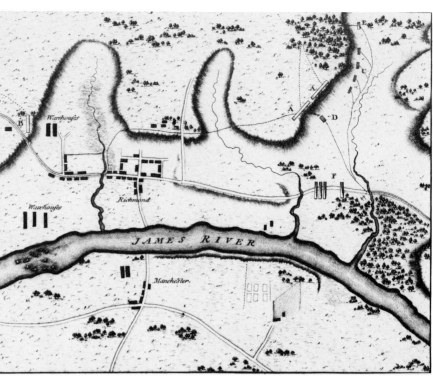

Warehouses

Warehouses

Richmond

Manchester

JAMES RIVER

5

6

War at Sea

1

2

The French navy's victory over the British in the battle of the Virginia capes on September 5, 1781, prevented Cornwallis's escape from Yorktown and assured allied victory. Under de Grasse, whom Washington called "the arbiter" of victory, the French outfought Britain's Admiral Thomas Graves (1). A French participant depicted the battle (2), and an English artist showed (3) an outnumbered British fleet, in foreground, attacking de Grasse, with Virginia's Eastern Shore in the background. A French map (4), published after Cornwallis's surrender, gave a bird's-eye view of the theater of war, with Cornwallis's seventy-five hundred troops penned up at Yorktown and Gloucester. The few British ships in the river were helpless against the French blockade stretched across the mouth of Chesapeake Bay.

3

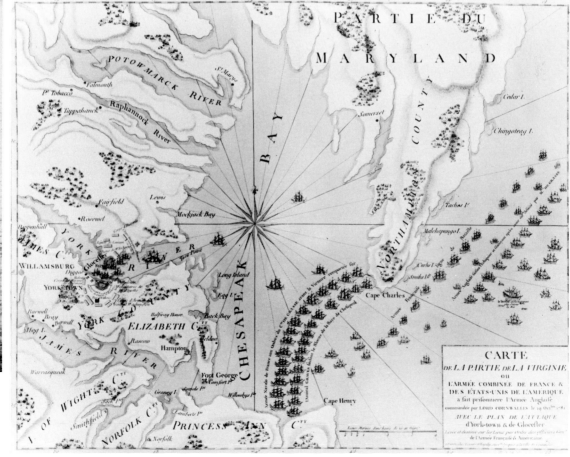

CARTE
DE LA PARTIE DE LA VIRGINIE
OÙ
L'ARMÉE COMBINÉE DE FRANCE &
DES ÉTATS-UNIS DE L'AMERIQUE
a fait prisonniere l'Armée Angloise
commandée par LORD CORNWALLIS le 19 Octobre 1781
AVEC LE PLAN DE L'ATTAQUE
d'York-town & de Glocester

PARTIE DU
MARYLAND

BAY

CHESAPEAK

POTOWMARCK RIVER

Raphannock River

JAMES Cy

YORK

WILLAMSBURG

YORK-TOWN

ELIZABETH Cy

I OF WIGHT Cy

NORFOLK Cy

PRINCESS ANN Cy

NORTHAMPTON COUNTY

Cape Charles

Cape Henry

Somerset

Cedar I.

Chingoteag I.

4

1

2

5

The allied victory at Yorktown realized America's hopes, but it left much of Virginia shattered. Artist James Peale painted Washington on the field (1), along with Lafayette, Knox, Rochambeau, Hamilton, and Tench Tilghman. Sunken British ships lie in the harbor. A detail of a panoramic view of the surrender on October 19, 1781 (2), shows British forces stripped of guns, marching from the surrender. One of the war's heroes was James Lafayette (3), a slave on a New Kent County plantation who served as body servant and spy for Lafayette. Freed for his efforts, he became an admired Richmond citizen. Yorktown was still a shambles (4) when emigrant English artist Benjamin Latrobe visited it in 1796; at left is the house of General Thomas Nelson, Jr., which had served as Cornwallis's headquarters. Above is the waterfront home of planter Augustine Moore (5), where the surrender was arranged by American, French, and British officers.

The British surrendered at Yorktown on October
19, 1781. Washington is shown at right rear.
Cornwallis although not actually at the ceremony
is at center, on a white horse.

1

3

2

MÉMOIRE

STATUTS ET PROSPECTUS,

CONCERNANT

L'ACADÉMIE

DES SCIENCES ET BEAUX-ARTS

DES ÉTATS-UNIS DE L'AMÉRIQUE,

ÉTABLIE A RICHEMOND,

CAPITALE DE LA VIRGINIE;

PRÉSENTÉS A LEURS MAJESTÉS,
ET A LA FAMILLE ROYALE,

Par le Chevalier QUESNAY DE BEAUREPAIRE.

A PARIS,

De l'Imprimerie de C A I L L E A U, *Imprimeur*
de l'Académie de R I C H E M O N D,
rue Gallande, Nº. 64.

1788.

4

Richmond became Virginia's capital in 1780. A temporary statehouse was established in the former Cuninghame and Sons warehouse (1), an abandoned business premise at Fourteenth and Canal streets. To educate Richmond's young men, French scholar Quesnay de Beaurepaire advertised his academy in 1788 (2); it soon closed, however. The town grew more imposing with the addition by 1789 of the Jeffersonian Capitol (3), seen in the engraving above from the James River. To guide Virginia's artisans, Jefferson had a plaster model (4) made in France of the Maison Carrée at Nimes, which he proposed as the form for the new statehouse. Facing south toward the James, the Capitol (5) was an imposing structure. It created a vogue for neoclassical architecture in the young Republic.

5

The Father of His Country

1

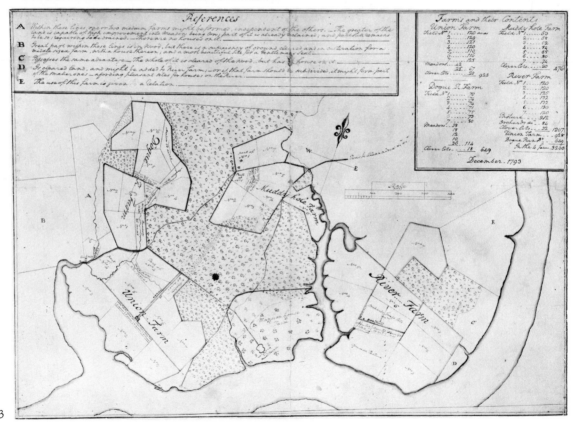

3

George Washington (1) was the hero of revolutionary America. Born to a modest planter family in Westmoreland County in 1732, he rose through a succession of military and civil accomplishments. On the death of his elder brother Lawrence, he inherited Mount Vernon (2) on the Potomac. A map (3), drawn by or for him in 1793, shows other farms he acquired, making him one of Virginia's greatest planters. In the kitchen (4) adjoining his house, a hearth and baking oven fed a steady succession of visiting kinsmen and friends. The dining room (5) was furnished with imported pieces, most of them from England. The artist Benjamin Latrobe painted Martha Washington serving tea on the portico (6) as sailing ships pass in the distance. When the "Father of His Country" died in 1799, many memorial paintings and drawings (7) were made, some of which were engraved and published. Washington was buried near his house, and passing ships tolled his death. Mount Vernon was acquired in the 1850s by the Mount Vernon Ladies' Association of the Union, led by Ann Pamela Cunningham of South Carolina. It remains open to the public.

6

7

1

2

3

Born eleven years after Washington, Thomas Jefferson (1) was of a more intellectual, artistic, and liberal nature. Brought up in Albemarle County, which was then close to Virginia's frontier of settlement, he shared many of the egalitarian views of the Scotch-Irish and Germanic frontiersmen who were his neighbors. He built Monticello (2), his plantation, over several decades, following the Italian style developed by Andrea Palladio. The west front of the house (3) looks toward the University of Virginia, which he created in his last years. Jefferson originally built his house without a dome (4), adding one later when funds permitted. He designed the university as an "academic village" centering around this classical rotunda (5). Flanking it were colonnades of one-story student accommodations, interrupted by handsome "pavilions" to house professors. Like Washington, Jefferson was buried close to his beloved house. His tombstone identifies him as penman of the Declaration of Independence, author of the Virginia Statute for Religious Freedom, and father of the University of Virginia.

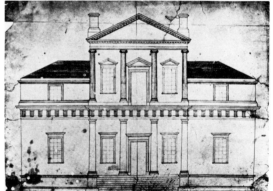

4

5

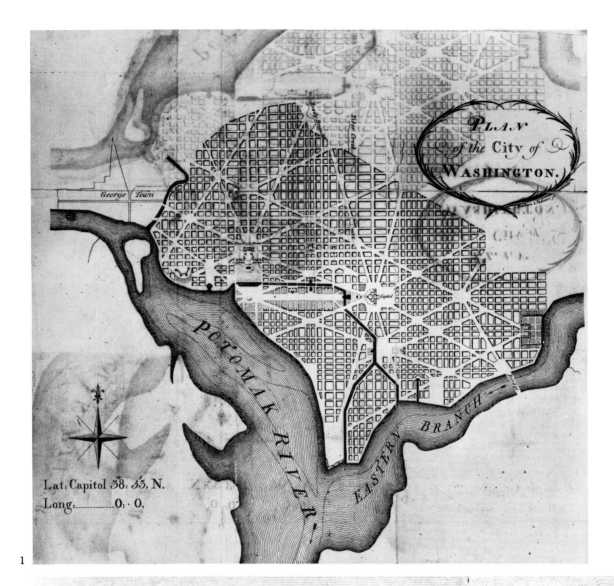

1

2

A Nation's Capital

Evidence of Virginia's pivotal role in the early Republic was Congress's decision to place the capital on the Potomac, between Virginia and Maryland. A new American age began in 1800 with the establishment of the muddy village of Washington (1). From the river, the early town (2) looked much like any Virginia seaport, linked by sailing ships with Atlantic ports, the Caribbean, and Europe. Fierce partisanship soon developed in the Republic, fanned in 1801 by the appointment of John Marshall (3), a leading Richmond attorney and friend of George Washington, as chief justice of the United States. Marshall and many of his friends continued to espouse the Federalist doctrines of Alexander Hamilton and John Adams. Strongly opposed to their centralism was Thomas Jefferson and his states' rights Republicans (later to be called Democrats), who included James Madison and James Monroe. In Richmond, the policies of Jefferson and his Virginia partisans were vigorously advanced by editor Thomas Ritchie in his *Richmond Enquirer,* while Federalist views, later to be represented by the Whigs, were supported by editor John Hampden Pleasants in the *Richmond Whig.* Virginia, the largest of the states, had ten members in the first House of Representatives, in 1789, as compared with eight each for Pennsylvania and Massachusetts and six for New York.

3

In Northern Virginia

With the decline of tobacco lands in the early Tidewater counties, prosperity moved northward and westward in Virginia. Among urban centers after the Revolution were Fredericksburg, established as a town in 1727; and Alexandria, planted by Scotch-Irishmen twenty-one years later. Alexandria was the trading center for such plantations as Mount Vernon and Gunston Hall. Its cobbled Prince Street (1) was lined with townhouses, some owned by wealthy planters. The town's Friendship Firehouse (2) was a volunteer organization whose membership included George Washington, who owned local property. The town's principal hostelry in these years was Gadsby's Tavern (3), on the main street. In nearby Fredericksburg lived Mary Ball Washington, mother of George, who spent her declining years in a house (4) which her son provided for her in 1772. A lawyer in post-revolutionary Fredericksburg was James Monroe, who began his practice here (5) in 1786.

1

In the eyes of the world, the word *Virginia* came to be synonymous with tobacco. Typical means of storing and transporting the "peculiar weed" were shown by William Tatham in his *Historical and Pictorial Essay,* published in 1800. Several types of drying and storing houses (1) used in eastern and southern Virginia included the log cabin, introduced to Virginia by Germanic settlers of the Valley. Tobacco hogsheads were transported by several methods (2), including dual-hull rafts, canal boats, wagons, and rolling hogsheads. After President Thomas Jefferson imposed an embargo against British shipping, an English cartoon (3) caricatured the ill effect on tobacco shippers of "Ograbme"—*embargo* spelled backward—here shown restraining a Virginia shipper from placing a hogshead aboard an outgoing British vessel. Virginia's economy was seriously hurt.

OGRABME, or. The American Snapping-turtle.

3

1

2

3

James Madison (1) was the ablest political theorist at the Constitutional Convention in 1787, proposing the Virginia Plan for a bicameral federal legislative body and other features incorporated in the Constitution. He married lively Dolley Payne Todd (2), a widow from Philadelphia. His cousin and namesake, the Reverend James Madison (3), was the first Episcopal bishop of Virginia and president of William and Mary College from 1777 to 1812. Succeeding Jefferson as president in 1809, Madison continued Jefferson's embargo on trade with Great Britain to protest British maritime offenses. During the ensuing War of 1812, the British demanded indemnity for losses suffered in Alexandria, Virginia, for which John Bull was caricatured in an American cartoon (4). British naval forces in 1813 entered Chesapeake Bay, pillaged Hampton, and went up the Potomac to lay waste to plantations and capture the city of Washington (5) on August 24, 1814. President and Mrs. Madison fled into Virginia to avoid capture. To prevent a recurrence of this sort of invasion, Congress in President Monroe's tenure authorized a dozen coastal forts, including Fortress Monroe.

99

1

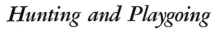

The thorough bred imported Horse,

Alderman,
Will stand the ensuing season, to cover mares at Mr. ISHAM BARROW's, in Halifax county. The terms of covering will be made known before the season commences.

THE NOTED HORSE
Dare-Devil,
Will stand the ensuing season, at my house in Chesterfield county.
THOMAS GOODE.

2

3

4

Much of life was spent outdoors, which remained placidly rural. John Randolph (1) of Roanoke plantation was depicted silhouetted in profile on his Southside acres among cavorting thoroughbreds of his stud. Newspaper advertisements (2) proclaimed the merits of Virginia racing sires. One of the earliest brought over from England was Monkey (3), imported by Nathaniel Harrison of Brandon, Prince George County, in 1737. In Virginia's few urban centers—Norfolk, Richmond, Petersburg, Alexandria—playgoing was popular, with traveling companies coming each winter from northern cities and occasionally from Great Britain. The nation was shocked in 1811 by the burning of Richmond's theater on Broad Street (4), resulting in the death of Governor George William Smith and sixty others. The playbill for the fatal performance (5) reveals the variety of theatrical fare offered in one long evening. As a result of the fire, many states passed laws requiring asbestos curtains and other fireproofing. On the site, Richmonders erected Monumental Episcopal Church, now the chapel of the Medical College of Virginia, as a memorial.

Last week of Performance this Season.

Mr. Placide's Benefit.

WILL CERTAINLY take place on

THURSDAY NEXT,

When will be presented, an entire New PLAY, translated from the French of Diderot, by a Gentleman of this City, called

THE FATHER;

OR,

FAMILY FEUDS.

| Monsieur Dubcsso,
St. Albin,
Commodore,
Germeul,
Le l'on,
Philip,
Le Bèe, | Mr. GREEN.
YOUNG.
THAITS.
ANDERSON.
BURKE.
ROSE.
DURANG. | Police Officer,
Duchemp,

Cecilia,
Sophia,
Clara,
Mrs. Herbert. | Mr. UTT.
HANNA.

Mrs. PLACIDE,
YOUNG.
Miss THOMAS.
Mrs UTT. |

At the End of the Play,

A COMIC SONG,	- - - By	- -	Mr. WEST.
A DANCE,	- - - - By	- - -	Miss E. PLACIDE.
SONG,	- - - - -	- -	Miss THOMAS.
A HORNPIPE,	- - - By	- -	Miss PLACIDE.

To which will be added, (for the first time here) the Favorite New Pantomime, of

Raymond and Agnes:

OR, THE BLEEDING NUN.

5

101

1

2

The fullest pictorial record of early Virginia was left by Germanic settlers of the uplands. In a series of engravings, the Shenandoah County settler Andrew Henkel, about 1810, showed family life (1) in the New Market area. In his *ABC Buch* (2), Henkel sprinkled English words among German ones to instruct the younger generation of families newly arrived from the Rhineland. Along the Appalachian settlement trail, Valley Germans made fraktur drawings, like other "Pennsylvania Germans;" the one at upper left, opposite (3), was issued by a Shenandoah County teacher, John Maphis, in 1848 as an award of merit to a student. Another Valley of Virginia fraktur (4) was made by Peter Bernhart in 1813 to record the birth in 1803 of Peter Brenneman, a Mennonite of Augusta or Rockingham County. A similar birth certificate (5), whose 1809 maker is unknown, shows Adam and Eve.

102

Monroe and Lafayette

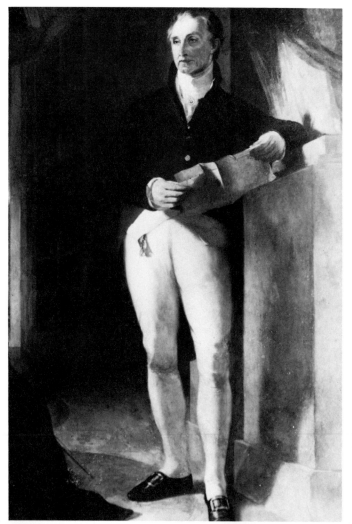

Like Washington and many of the Lees, James Monroe (1) was born in Westmoreland County. He became the fifth president in 1817, the fourth of the "Virginia dynasty" begun with Washington. Monroe lived for a time at the site of Ash Lawn (2), near Charlottesville. Built at his instigation during the War of 1812 period was Bellona Arsenal (3), in Chesterfield County, one of several state-supported military bases intended to protect Virginia against attack. In 1824, Virginia welcomed the aging Lafayette back to Yorktown, Williamsburg, Richmond, and other Revolutionary War sites. An imprint on silk (4), issued in Richmond, shows Lafayette being crowned with laurels over a view of "Cornwallis Resigning his Sword at York Town." A woodcut (5) depicts the Frenchman's arrival in a chaise to the huzzas of a stylishly dressed crowd. Elaborate testimonial dinners were held at Williamsburg's Raleigh Tavern and in Richmond.

LA FAYETTE

CORNWALLIS
Resigning his Sword at York Town, October 19th 1781.

Sold at *Raymond & Brothers* Universal Hat Warehouse,
Richmond Va.

Copy Right Secured.

WELCOME LA FAYETTE

Pressed by western Virginians for a greater role in its government, Virginia held a constitutional convention in 1829–30. Called "the Last Meeting of the Giants," the convention brought forth

many celebrities. Shown in this painting by George Catlin are James Monroe, in the president's chair; James Madison, standing; John Tyler, clockwise from the president's chair, twentieth in the second row; John Marshall, eighteenth in the first row; and John Randolph of Roanoke, second in the second row.

1

2

Nineteenth-century Richmond gained much of the social and intellectual luster that Williamsburg had enjoyed. The neoclassical State Capitol dominates the skyline of this idyllic view (1), made in 1833 from the heights along the James River, west of the Capitol. As Richmond grew, its early inns and rooming houses gave way to the handsome Exchange Hotel (2), where many famous visitors were housed and many banquets served before the Civil War. The city's rival newspapers were the *Enquirer,* which was Democratic, and the *Whig,* which espoused conservative views. Newspaper advertisements opposite (3) reveal various aspects of life in nineteenth-century Virginia.

Gordonsville for Sale.

THE subscriber offers for sale his Tavern at Gordonsville, in Orange county, with 250 acres of Land attached to it, or to exchange it for property in the city of Richmond. Gordonsville is situated at the foot of the Southwest Mountains, 21 miles from the University of Virginia, 50 from Fredericksburg, 50 from Harrisonburg, and 70 miles from this place. The stages from Charlottesville to Fredericksburg pass three time a week, and since the late arrangement of the mails between Staunton and Guyandott, the number of passengers has greatly increased. The mail stage from Richmond to Harrisonburg passes twice a week. For terms and farther particulars, apply to the subscriber. JOHN N. GORDON.

Richmond, 24th Sept. ts

FRESH GOODS.

RECEIVED by the Exit, from New York, very superior black Mandarin and French crapes; black and coloured Italian nets; Italian lutestrings and Gros de Naples; a superior assortment of ginghams and calicoes; plain and worked Swiss muslins; laces and edgings, lace capes and veils; gloves; ribbons, and a variety of other goods, for sale at reduced prices for cash, by HALL NEILSON.

aug 18

3

1

Academies and Free Schools

Lacking public education until 1870, Virginians chiefly depended on their parents and ministers for schooling. But there were a few early schools. Benjamin Hallowell, a Quaker, had a school (1) in Alexandria, educating young Robert E. Lee, among many others. At Hampton, the Syms-Eaton Free School (2) merged two seventeenth-century free schools that had been endowed by English immigrants. Especially education-minded were the Scotch-Irish, who came into the Valley of Virginia after 1720. An early Augusta County school was Mossy Creek Academy (3), which operated before the Civil War. An important figure in Virginia education was William Barton Rogers (4), a scientist at William and Mary and the University of Virginia who later founded the Massachusetts Institute of Technology. Another was Nathaniel Beverley Tucker (5), who succeeded his father, St. George Tucker, as professor of law at William and Mary. Along with a few other denominational colleges and the University of Virginia, the Williamsburg college (6) trained planters' sons in classical studies.

2

3

4

5

6

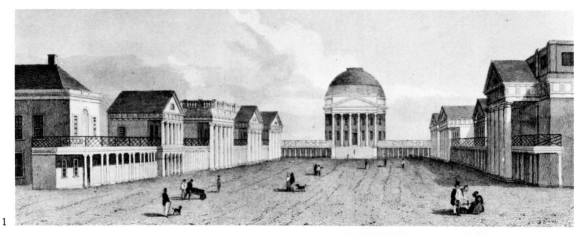

The lawn of the University of Virginia (1), laid out by Jefferson, was complete by 1830. Early professors at Charlottesville were John B. Minor, law (2); William Holmes McGuffey (3), author of the famous schoolbooks, *McGuffey's Readers;* and Socrates Maupin, who taught science (4). Virginia Military Institute (5) grew in 1839 from the state arsenal at Lexington. Randolph-Macon College (6) was begun in 1830 by Methodists at Boydton but was later moved to Ashland. Washington College (7) evolved in the early 1800s at Lexington from a log cabin academy begun by Scotch-Irishmen in Augusta County in 1749; it was endowed by George Washington with fifty thousand dollars in canal stock, and it was renamed Washington and Lee University after Robert E. Lee served as president following the Civil War.

5

6

7

Order
OF THE
COLLEGIATE EXERCISES
ON THE
4th of July.

INTRODUCTORY PRAYER.

ORATIONS.

1. EULOGY ON *Thomas Jefferson*—by Thos. Martin.
2. ORATION ON *Ancient and Modern Literature*—by C. Q. Tompkins.
3. " *On Modern improvements in Natural Philosophy*—by George W. Semple.
*4. " *On the History and Advantages of Commerce*—by Edmund P. Oliver.
*5. " *On the Influence of our Retrospective Emotions upon our present condition and future views*—by Jno. D. Munford.
*6. " *On the Profession of the Law*—by Jas. N. McPherson.
7. " *On the Art of Printing and the Advantages of a Free Press*—by Ro. Ridley.
8. " *On the influence of Luxury upon the Social and Political condition of Man*—by Wm. W. Wingfield.
9. " *On Honour*—by Alfred Johns.
*10. " *On American Jurisprudence*—by Edward Simmons.
11. " *On the True Glory of a Nation*—by James B. Watts.
12. " *On the Influence of the Arts and Sciences upon the Moral and Political Condition of Mankind*—by Cyrus A. Griffin.
13. " *On the comparative merits of the Warrior and Philosopher*—by Edward I. Young.
14. " *On the Progress of Civilization and the Present Prospects of the World*—by Geo. Blow.
15. " *On the Day*—by Thomas H. Daniel.

Degrees delivered to the Candidates by the President.

Baccalaureate Address.

CONCLUDING PRAYER.

N. B.—The Asterisk designates those who are absent from town, and those who, though present, have been prevented, by indisposition, from preparing for the public exercises.

1

Graduation Day

In the early years of the nineteenth century, educational opportunities were few. William and Mary taught a select few, graduating them at ceremonies

2

like those listed in its 1831 program (1). Miss
Betty Carter's Seminary in Chesterfield County (2)
was a finishing school of the same period.

1

2

Arise! Arise! and weep no more
dry up your tears, we shall part
no more. Come rose we go to
Tennessee,
that happy Shore. To old virginia
never — never — return. —

With the rise of abolitionism in the North, slavery became a violent issue. The emigrant English artist Benjamin Latrobe portrayed an overseer supervising two slaves near Fredericksburg (1). Violence erupted in Southampton County in 1831 when slave Nat Turner led an insurrection (2) which resulted in the killing of white masters and their families. The illustration is from *An Authentic and Impartial Narrative . . .* published in 1831 in New York. Slaves being led by white guards (3) from Staunton along the Great Wagon Road into Tennessee about mid-century were sketched by itinerant artist Lewis Miller. At Christiansburg, Miller sketched the auction of three blacks (4), a scene he encountered on a return to his birthplace in Montgomery County. In his *Collected History of Virginia,* published in 1854, historian Henry Howe depicted slave quarters behind a Virginia farm (5); the master's son plays with black children while a slave woman carries a burden in a head basket.

2

3

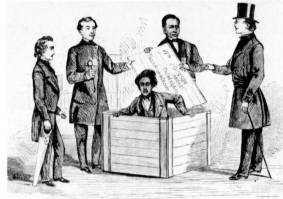

4

The effects of slavery, the South's "peculiar institution," permeated life. Slaves are shown harvesting wheat (1) at Mount Vernon in an 1851 painting by Junius Brutus Stearns. A Civil War photograph shows the slave market of Price, Birch & Co. at Alexandria (2). Another photograph shows the inside of a slave pen at Alexandria (3). With the aid of abolitionists in Virginia and northward, many slaves escaped and were spirited by the "Underground Railway" to freedom. "The Resurrection of Henry Box Brown" (4), printed in the North, depicted the arrival in Philadelphia in 1850 of a fugitive Richmond slave who had been placed in a box and sent to Pennsylvania. A few freed slaves lived in Virginia, but Virginia emancipationists encouraged emigration of blacks to Liberia. John Marshall and James Monroe were leaders of the movement to repatriate the Africans; but the movement was opposed by many slaveholders.

The Growth of Cities

Dominantly rural, Virginia had few cities. One of the fastest to grow was Alexandria (1), seen in an 1844 view. Many townscapes were included in *Howe's Collected History of Virginia,* published in 1854 in Charleston, S.C. Among those depicted were Fredericksburg (2), as viewed across the Rappahannock River from Ferry Farm, where George Washington once lived; Petersburg (3), an important tobacco and rail center on the Appomattox River; Abingdon (4), one of the first and most urbane of western Virginia towns, developed as the seat of early Campbell County; and Lynchburg (5), built on the site of Lynch's Ferry, across the upper James. It was Virginia's largest western town in these years.

PAGES 122–123: The city of Danville.

4

5

1

2

3

4

5

6

Pilot boats were increasingly used in Chesapeake Bay as ship commerce grew. The pilot vessel *Mary of Norfolk* (1) was depicted in 1815. A capacious dry dock (2) was opened in 1833 at Portsmouth, where a U.S. Navy Yard had developed. By 1845 Norfolk had extensive dockside markets (3) to handle cargo from Virginia, Carolina, and Caribbean ports. In 1854 Henry Howe showed the entrance to Norfolk and Portsmouth harbors (4). The view was made from Fort Norfolk. A close-up of Portsmouth's harbor in 1843 (5) was dominated by a U.S. Navy man-of-war, which was surrounded by lesser vessels; at right is the Naval Hospital. Built in the Navy Yard at Portsmouth was the U.S.S. *Delaware,* which was launched in 1817; a bronze reproduction (6) of the original carved bowsprit, depicting an Indian, stands at the Naval Academy in Annapolis.

125

1

Picturesque Virginia

Scenic beauty was depicted in many books and prints issued in nineteenth-century America and Europe. In the beautiful *Album of Virginia*, done by Edward Beyer and printed in Dresden in 1857, "Rockfish Gap and the Mountain House" (1) is shown as a double-page spread. The lithograph shows the gap in the Blue Ridge Mountains at Afton frequently used in travel between Charlottesville and Staunton; a century later, the Skyline Drive was created along the mountain range by the National Park Service. Another scenic favorite was Natural Bridge (2) between Lexington and Lynchburg, which inspired the name of Rockbridge County. A stagecoach route crossed the limestone bridge, which was commonly called one of the seven wonders of the modern world. Caverns exerted romantic appeal to travelers in the Valley of Virginia. A print of Weyer's Cave (3), later called Grand Caverns, shows a guide pointing out features to sightseers holding lanterns.

2

3

1

2

3

4

Exotic vistas and mineral springs attracted travelers in search of novelty. Upland Virginia offered a number of spas, whose waters were recommended for a variety of ills. Among them were White Sulphur Springs in Montgomery County. The handsome resort, depicted by Edward Beyer in 1854 in his *Album of Virginia* (1), consisted of a central fountain of spring water surrounded by bridle paths and hotels and dormitories for summer guests. In Bath County were the Warm Springs (2), where bathing pools for men and women (carefully separated) were considered helpful for rheumatic ailments. Nearby in Bath County was Bath Alum Springs (3), where President John Tyler sojourned. Farther south, in Dismal Swamp on the North Carolina line near Suffolk, travelers through Dismal Swamp Canal often stopped at Lake Drummond Hotel (4). "Fortress Monroe, Old Point Comfort and Hygeia Hotel, Va.," (5) provided visitors with invigorating sea air.

5

1

Portsmouth & Roanoke
RAIL ROAD.
THE LOCOMOTIVE En-
gine JOHN BARNETT, with its train of
Coaches & Cars, will commence running
between *Portsmouth* and *Suffolk* on Wed-
nesday, 24th inst.—Leaving Portsmouth
daily at 8 A. M. and 3 P. M. and Suffolk at
10 A. M. and 4 P. M.

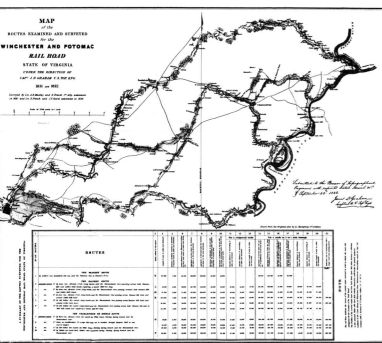

MAP
of the
ROUTES EXAMINED AND SURVEYED
for the
WINCHESTER AND POTOMAC
RAIL ROAD
STATE OF VIRGINIA
UNDER THE DIRECTION OF
CAPT. J. D. GRAHAM U.S. TOP. ENG.
1831 AND 1832

3

4

The building of railroads revolutionized transport in Virginia. One early route (1) connected
Portsmouth with the inland town of Suffolk some
twenty miles away. Before the coming of the
railroad, riverside towns such as Columbia (2) in
Fluvanna County enjoyed an advantage. An
1832 map (3) shows the countryside that would
be opened up by the construction of a railroad
between Winchester and the Potomac River. Another revolution occurred in 1831 with the invention of a wheat reaper by Cyrus McCormick
(4), a Virginia farmer. McCormick's first reaper
(5) was built in his workshop (6) at Raphine,
north of Lexington.

5

6

1

2

3

Richmond's Industry

Richmond (1), shown here in an 1852 lithograph, benefited from the creation of the James River Canal system, westward to Lynchburg. The Tredegar Iron Works (2) were built on the James at Richmond to make rails and machinery. From the select residential area called Gamble's Hill, artist Edward Beyer sketched this panoramic view (3) of the nearby canal, with its horses and barges, and the great Virginia Manufactory of Arms. Beyond, Mayo's Bridge spanned the James to Manchester, on the south shore, later to become South Richmond. One of Virginia's first banks was the Farmers' Bank of Richmond (4), shown at left of the U.S. Customs House and Treasury Building on Richmond's Main Street before the Civil War. Richmonders were sketched in a barber shop (5) by the English artist Eyre Crowe.

4

5

1

2

3

Exchange Hotel.
RICHMOND, VA.

DINNER IN HONOR OF MR. STEVENSON.

BILL OF FARE.

Mock Turtle Soup.   Boiled Leg Mutton.
Rock Fish à la Chambord.   Do. Ham.
Chub, Capre Sauce.   Do. Tongue.

COLD DISHES.
Galantine Turkey, mounted.   Oysters in Jelly, mounted.
Bread of Chickens.   Cold Game Pie, with Truffles.

12 ENTREES.
Turban of Filets of Hare.
Chickens Legs with Mushrooms.
Arcade of Filets of Chicken.
Chicken Pie à la Financier, with Truffles.
Mutton Cutlets à la Soubise.
Croustade of Supreme of Chicken.
Calf's Brains au Souffel.
Filets of Partridges au fumie de jibier.
Timbale of Macaroni.
Mayonaise of Chicken, with Jelly.
Calf's Head en Tortue.
Vol au Vent à la Toulouse.

ROASTS.
Roast Beef.   Roast Goose.
Do. Saddle of Mutton.   Do. Ducks.
Do. Leg of Mutton.   Do. Chickens.
Roast Turkey.

GAME.
Saddle of Venison.   Wild Ducks.
Wild Turkey.   Teal.
Do. Goose.   Partridges.

VEGETABLES.
Mashed Potatoes.   Spinage.
Plain   do.   Brocoli.
Sweet   do.   Salsifits.
Green French Peas.   Turnips.
Hominy.

DESSERT.
Cabinet Pudding.   Ice Cream.
Charlotte Russe.   Blanc Mange.
Jelly Russe Marasquino.   Rum Jelly.
Biscuit de Savoie.   Nugat.
Gateaux Milles Fieulles.   Petits Gateaux à la Parisienne.
Petites Bouchées à la Royale. Batons à la Canelle.
Champignons.   Meringues à la Crème.
Bouchées des dames.   Couronnes d'Armandes.
Risolles of Quince.

FRUIT.

Coffee and Liqueur.

EXCHANGE HOTEL, 11th *December*, 1841.

BERNARD, PRINTER, MUSEUM BUILDING.

4

THE VIRGINIANS

A TALE OF THE LAST CENTURY.

BY W. M. THACKERAY.

Author of "Esmond,"
"Vanity Fair,"
"The Newcomes,"
&c. &c.

LONDON:
BRADBURY AND EVANS, 11, BOUVERIE STREET.
1857.

Richmond was important as the capital of a major state. A notable Richmond political figure was President John Tyler (1), of Charles City County, a onetime legislator, governor, and U.S. senator. Another was Andrew Stevenson of Albemarle (2), onetime Speaker of the House of Representatives, who was honored at a banquet at the Exchange Hotel in 1841 (3). An old Richmond dwelling was the house of Jacob Ege (4), later a museum honoring the Richmond writer Edgar Allan Poe (5). Other writers who visited Richmond were Charles Dickens (6) and William Thackeray, who wrote *The Virginians* (7) in 1857.

The Jamestown Celebration

As bitterness built toward Civil War, Virginia in 1857 proudly celebrated the 150th anniversary of the arrival of the first permanent English settlers in the New World. An article in *Harper's Weekly* described a great gathering of ships, and a great ceremony on the shore at Jamestown, by then a deserted island in the James River. A visiting artist sketched crewmen loading the cannon for a salute (1). Another *Harper's* view showed a sidewheeler and other excursion boats gathered in the river (2), while a celebrator drank from a jug near cypress trees on shore. Thousands of troops gathered (3) for a parade and for military honors in the presence of Virginia's Governor Henry A. Wise of Accomack. The next day, Jamestown was again virtually deserted.

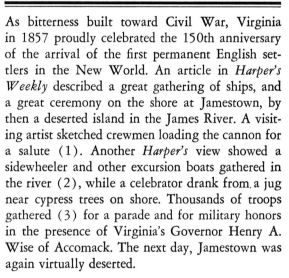

1

2

Although Virginia was originally Anglican, other denominations became prominent after 1800. Episcopal leaders included Bishops Richard Channing Moore (1), who served from 1818 to 1841, and William Meade (2), who infused zeal from 1841 to 1862. The Monumental Episcopal Church was built on the site of Richmond's theater fire of 1811; originally planned with a steeple, it was left steepleless (3). Reverend Moses Hoge (4) was head of Hampden-Sydney from 1807 to 1820 and father of a famous preacher. Richmond's First Baptist Church (5) started in 1802 in modest form. In the manse of Staunton's First Presbyterian Church (6), Woodrow Wilson was born in 1856.

3

Moses Hoge

4

5

6

Antislavery feeling mounted in the 1850s as the North and West joined forces in Congress. Governor Henry Wise (1) sought to moderate extremism throughout Virginia, but John Brown's (2) capture of the Harper's Ferry arsenal in the northern section of the state in 1859 aroused the South. After the arsenal had been stormed and captured (3) by Marines and Brown taken under military arrest by a U.S. Army force under Major Robert E. Lee (4), Brown was tried at Charles Town for treason and murder (5). Convicted, the zealous firebrand was carted to the gallows (6), seated on his coffin, and bound with rope, while soldiers walked alongside the wagon to prevent an escape or demonstration. Hanged in public (7), John Brown was hailed by northern abolitionists as a martyr, while in the South he was viewed as a madman. The incident served to widen the breach between sections. Churches split into northern and southern wings, and political parties disintegrated. Despite the efforts of moderate Virginians to allay growing sectional feeling, the nation was headed inevitably toward division.

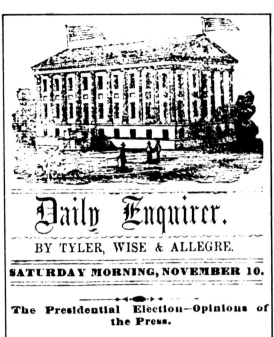

7

The Presidential Election—Opinions of the Press.

That this condition of things brings the country, and necessarily so, into the jaws of fearful convulsions, is, we think, perfectly certain. To state this is but to restate what distinguished men of all parties, in the North and in the South, have again and again laid down as axiomatic truths.

Daily Enquirer.

BY TYLER, WISE & ALLEGRE.

SATURDAY MORNING, NOVEMBER 10.

1

2

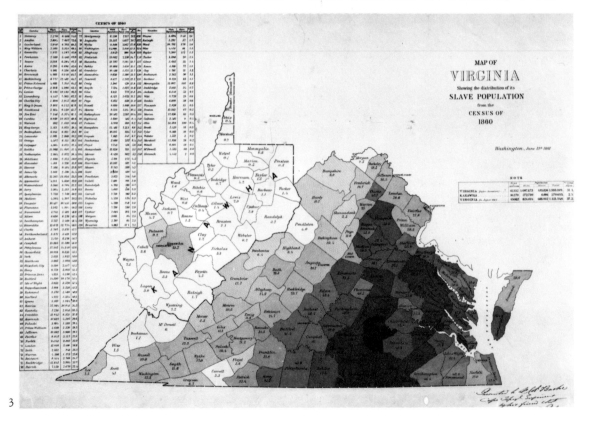

3

Virginia was reluctant to follow the secessionist lead of South Carolina. However, Abraham Lincoln's election as president in 1860 led the *Richmond Daily Enquirer* (1) to predict "fearful convulsions." Governor John Letcher (2), of Lexington, called a convention in Richmond after the firing on Fort Sumter in an effort to mediate the national crisis. But after Lincoln called on Virginia to help put down secession, the convention voted to secede. The Secession Ordinance was supported by eastern Virginia and the Piedmont region—where slaveholding was general, as shown on a contemporary map (3)—but opposed by some western delegates. Among strategic sites seized by Federal troops in Virginia was Arlington House (4), home of Robert E. Lee's father-in-law, across the Potomac from the District of Columbia. Virginia hurriedly increased its military forces in fear of federal invasion. A typical commission, given James Innes Randolph (5) as a second lieutenant in the Provisional Army of Virginia, was signed by Governor John Letcher on July 8, 1861.

4

Commonwealth of Virginia.

To *James Innis Randolph* Greeting:

Know You, That from special trust and confidence reposed in your fidelity, courage and good conduct, our GOVERNOR, in pursuance of the authority vested in him by an Ordinance of the Convention of the State of Virginia, doth commission you a

Second Lieutenant (for Engineer duty)

in the PROVISIONAL ARMY of the State of Virginia, to rank as such from the *Eighth* day of *May* 18*61*.

In testimony whereof, I have hereunto signed my name as Governor, and caused the Seal of the Commonwealth to be affixed, this *8th* day of *July* 186*1*.

John Letcher

5

The Seat of War

Two months after Virginia seceded, *Harper's
Weekly* published this "pictorial map of the seat of
war, showing parts of the states of Maryland, Delaware, Virginia, and North Carolina, and also the
coast line from Cape Henry to Fort Pickens, with
the United States' blockading fleet." Because of its
proximity to the District of Columbia, Virginia was
the principal theater of the war, from the Peninsula
campaign of 1862 until Lee's surrender at Appomattox three years later.

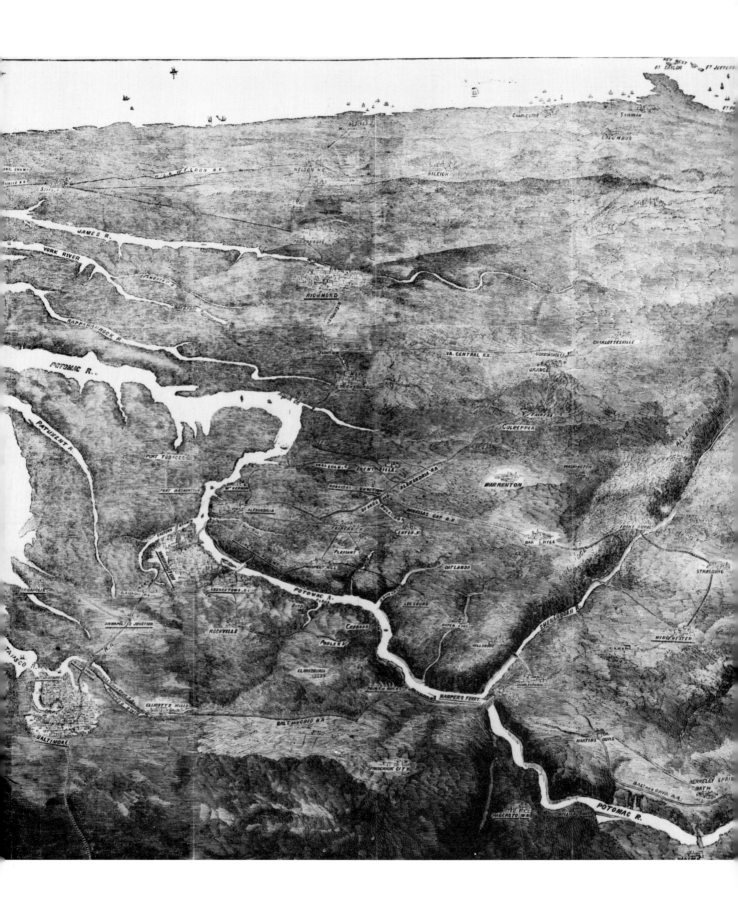

1

2

3

Richmond was derided as "the capital of the rebel government" in the northern press, but it assumed new importance in the world. The capital of the Confederacy soon moved there from Montgomery, and Broad Street (1) became a busy thoroughfare. President of the Confederate States was Jefferson Davis of Mississippi (2), who had been trained as a soldier at West Point. The Davises occupied the porticoed house (3) overlooking Shockoe Valley, which had once been the home of Dr. John Brockenbrough, president of the Bank of Virginia. Widely depicted as "the Capital of the Confederacy" was Virginia's Capitol (4). Fort Monroe, at Old Point Comfort, remained in U.S. Army hands and became a haven for fugitive slaves (5), who were given food and shelter and assigned work building defenses.

1

2

When Virginia seceded from the Union, federal forces strengthened some of their naval and military bases in the state, while abandoning others. On April 18, 1861, they burned the important U.S. arsenal at Harper's Ferry (1), shown abandoned in foreground in this print. Also destroyed by federal command was the Portsmouth Navy Yard (2), together with its dry docks and ship lofts. Among the naval ships destroyed at the same time was the forty-gun U.S.S. *Merrimack* (3), shown ablaze with other vessels in a holocaust that destroyed $35 million worth of federal property. The *Merrimack*'s hull was used by the Confederates in constructing their ironclad C.S.S. *Virginia,* which was to battle the U.S.S. *Monitor* in the world's first ironclad combat in Hampton Roads not long afterward. Still held by the U.S. Army was powerful Fort Monroe, at Old Point Comfort, which Confederates called "a dagger in the heart of the Confederacy."

A bird's-eye view of Fort Monroe before the Civil War (1) shows the Hygeia Hotel alongside it and sailing ships surrounding it. On May 22, 1861, Union General Benjamin Butler arrived and took command of union fortifications on the Peninsula's tip. From Monroe's stronghold (2), General John Wool soon crossed Hampton Roads to Ocean View and forced the Confederates to evacuate Norfolk. To prevent federal use of nearby Hampton, Confederates burned it in 1861 (3). The start of the Union's abortive Peninsula campaign was signaled by the arrival from Washington in 1862 of General George B. McClellan's Army of the Potomac (4), shown marching past the Hygeia Hotel after landing at Fort Monroe. The first battle of the war was at Little Bethel, near Hampton. A picture of "Colonel Duryea's regiment ferried over Hampton Creek . . . to attack secession forces at Little Bethel . . ." (5) was printed in *Frank Leslie's Illustrated Newspaper.*

3

4

5

At Bull Run and Ball's Bluff

1

2

Despite its huge advantage in size and equipment, the Union gained few early victories in the Civil War. In the first battle of Bull Run (1) in 1861, a federal attack was met by General Jackson "standing like a stone wall." Similarly, Union forces were driven back by Confederates in the battle of Ball's Bluff in Loudoun County a few months later, as portrayed in *The Illustrated London News* (2). The Confederacy's direst problem was lack of equipment; a Virginia infantryman (3) holds a sword and flintlock rifle, the latter made in Virginia. At the Tredegar Iron Works in Richmond (4), metal gun carriages were forged by hand. Sometimes material was so scarce that dummy guns were made and placed in position to fool the enemy. One such gun (5) was left behind when Virginia troops evacuated a post at Centerville.

MAKING GUN CARRIAGES of the RICHMOND ARMORY

4

5

The Mayor & Councils of Norfolk meeting the federal forces under a flag of truce

The Council Tree

Hoisting the old flag on the Custom house

Entering the City of Norfolk

Burning of the Gosport Navy-Yard

Federal forces captured Norfolk (1) on May 10, 1862; "Scenes of the Occupation" were shown in *Harper's Weekly.* A Confederate ironclad, the *Yorktown* (2), tried to break through the James River blockade but was driven back. More successful was the Confederate *Virginia,* built on the *Merrimack*'s hull, which sank the U.S.S. *Cumberland* (3) off Newport News on March 8, 1862. The historic battle between the *Monitor* and the *Virginia,* marking the beginning of the age of ironclad ships, was fought in Hampton Roads next day, midway between Norfolk and Newport News. After neither ship proved able to sink the other, the battle ended in a draw. The crew of the U.S.S. *Monitor* (4) was photographed on the deck of the "cheese box on a raft" by Mathew Brady, famed Civil War photographer.

OVERLEAF: The battle between the *Virginia* and the *Monitor.*

The Peninsula

Virginia soon became the battleground of the Civil War. General George B. McClellan (1) landed troops at Fort Monroe and Newport News, hoping to move up the Peninsula to capture Richmond. A print (2) shows McClellan's army moving from Big Bethel, near Hampton, toward Yorktown. An aide to General McClellan was young Captain George Custer (3), recently out of West Point. Named by Virginia to command the state's defending army was General Joseph E. Johnston (4), born in Prince Edward County and educated at West Point; after an injury, however, Johnston was succeeded by Robert E. Lee. Winslow Homer painted this watercolor of "Reconnaissance in force by Gen'l Gorman before Yorktown" (5) for a northern newspaper. After taking Yorktown in 1862, federal forces fortified it (6), using siege lines dug by Cornwallis's defending British forces there in 1781.

B-5867

2

3

4

Reconnoissance in force by Genl Gorman before Yorktown.
Rebel Battery only three hundred yards distant behind the woods

1

2

3

The war was a mixture of terror, pain, humor, and endless boredom. Virginia artist Conrad Wise Chapman depicted himself in "Picket Post" (1). In the important battle of Seven Pines, near Richmond (2), southern forces turned back McClellan's drive on Richmond. The fighting around Richmond erupted again in the battle of Gaines's Mill (3); Captain DeHart's federal battery, shown here, shelled a Confederate advance on June 27, 1862. McClellan's field hospital and salvage station (4) were photographed after the battle of Gaines's Mill. Dissatisfied by McClellan's cautious conduct of his campaign, President Lincoln came to Berkeley plantation in July 1862 and met with McClellan after a military review of federal troops (5). McClellan was soon replaced.

4

5

Union Advances

Union forces struck rapidly to capture northern Virginia towns and protect the District of Columbia. A month after Virginia had seceded, federal troops marched into Alexandria (1), filing down the road from Washington (2). Federal forces were soon installed in major public buildings (3). Alexandria's port (4) was used to load troops headed into Tidewater Virginia to take part in General George B. McClellan's Peninsula Campaign. To halt this movement, Confederate batteries were installed on the Potomac (5) at the mouth of Aquia Creek; from there they bombarded Union warships headed downriver to the Chesapeake Bay and thence up the James, the York, and the Pamunkey rivers. Most warships were fitted with both sails and engines, for by this time the invention of steam propulsion had almost revolutionized shipping.

3

4

5

A familiar figure to Confederates was Lee on Traveller, his sorrel horse; this popular photograph (1) was made by Michael Miley after the war in Lexington, when Lee was president of Washington College. Many Union soldiers were imprisoned in Richmond's Libby Prison (2), a former warehouse near Chimborazo Hill used by Confederates for prisoners of war; this scene was painted by David Gilmour Blyth. The outside of Libby Prison (3) was patrolled by Confederates; at right in the lithograph, the James River and a railroad bridge can be seen. "General Sigel's [Union] Corps at the Second Battle of Bull Run" was shown in *Harper's Weekly* for September 20, 1862. After the abortive Peninsula campaign of 1862, Confederate soldiers were photographed (5) in winter quarters at Manassas, near Fredericksburg.

Stonewall Jackson

Next to Lee in popular affection came Thomas Jonathan ("Stonewall") Jackson, the South's most able tactician. He was photographed (1) early in the war, with his new beard. Jackson's field cap and handkerchief (2) are shown in Richmond's Confederate Museum, along with the hat, sword, field glasses, and pistol (3) of another Confederate hero, General James Ewell Brown ("Jeb") Stuart, who was akin to Jackson in daring. In his historic Valley campaign, Jackson gained the respect of both sides and became a hero to many Europeans. Jackson's army is shown defeating the Union at Winchester (4) in 1862. A few months later, Jackson won the battle of Cross Keys (5). The great soldier was mistakenly shot by his own men the next year in the battle of Chancellorsville (6) and died soon afterward.

1

2

3

4

1

From Richmond

2

3

U. S. COURT ROOM, ALEXANDRIA, VA.,
JULY 23rd, 1864.

TO THE COLORED MEN
OF VIRGINIA.

The undersigned offers to a limited number of able-bodied and brave men, who are willing to enlist in the service of the United States for one year.

A BOUNTY OF $200 EACH,

to be paid when mustered into the service.

Each man will also receive **ANOTHER HUNDRED DOLLARS** from the United States, besides **Sixteen Dollars per month and Rations,** making for the years' service, about

FIVE HUNDRED DOLLARS AND RATIONS.

Every man will in this way be able to secure a comfortable home for himself and family, to be his and theirs forever; and all will also be able to show their gratitude to the Government for the

BOON OF FREEDOM NOW ENJOYED,

And in many cases they will have the pleasure of restoring to home and freedom, brothers and sisters, and fathers and mothers who in years past were torn from them by the cruel traders and sold to the far South.

The undersigned will also aid all who enlist in procuring homes for their families, and will attend to the business at his **Office, in the Upper Story of the Post Office Building.**

JOHN C. UNDERWOOD,
U. S. District Judge.

Virginia's Resources

Virginia's resources were utilized by invading northern troops almost as much as by the South's defenders. Wounded federal soldiers (1) were treated in makeshift hospitals before leaving the battle zone. The hospital shown here (2) was formerly a warehouse. Efforts were made to attract Virginia's ex-slaves into federal ranks after Lincoln's Emancipation Proclamation; a broadside (3) offered monetary rewards for enlistments. The ruined Norfolk Navy Yard (4), photographed after federal forces had burned it in 1861, was utilized as a federal base, and some of the shops that had been burned were rebuilt.

4

At Fredericksburg

4

Fredericksburg was a crucial port and rail center, fought over bitterly in the Civil War. Even after being bombed (1), it looked deceptively serene, although the rail bridge in the foreground had been destroyed. The bombing of the town (2) by the Union Army of the Potomac was shown in *Frank Leslie's Illustrated Newspaper*. But inside the town the ruins (3) appeared ghastly after Union bombardment. *The Illustrated London News* carried this view (4) of Union siege troops. Many Confederates (5) were killed defending the town. An observer entering Fredericksburg with the Union conquerors found the town "utterly desolate." Federal troops in Tidewater Virginia were supplied by federal gunboats from Washington, which came up the Pamunkey River to White House (6), near the present West Point.

5

6

1

2

3

In the midst of the war, Virginia was split by a secession of its own. In June 1861, Union adherents of western counties met in Wheeling (1) and voted to withdraw from Virginia. Although this was opposed by the state as unconstitutional, it was recognized as legal by Congress, and West Virginia was admitted to the Union in 1863. Francis Pierpont (2) was elected governor by the "restored" government in 1863, and Lemuel Bowden (3), a Williamsburg attorney, was chosen as a U.S. senator, though he died after brief service. Virginia's Confederate government issued handbills (4) warning Unionists they would be punished by death. In September 1863, the important "Wilderness Road" from western Virginia through Cumberland Gap was captured (5) by a Union army under General Ambrose Burnside. Holding the Baltimore & Ohio Railroad from Maryland into West Virginia was a powerful Union advantage; one historian wrote that West Virginia's secession was secretly maneuvered by the Union to keep the railway in federal hands.

TREASON IN VIRGINIA.

The Code of Virginia defines treason to be

"In levying war against the State, adhering to its enemies, or giving them aid and comfort."

Such treason, if proved by two witnesses, is punishable by death.

MAY 15, 1861.

4

5

Heroes and Heroines

Belle Boyd (1) of Virginia was a famous spy for the Confederacy during Jackson's whirlwind campaigns in the Valley of Virginia; she began serving as a southern courier at the age of seventeen. A Unionist spy in Richmond was Elizabeth Van Lew (2), shown outside her mansion on Church Hill, overlooking the James and its canal. A popular Confederate print was "The Burial of Latane" (3), showing a Virginia soldier being buried by sad women, children, and servants on a plantation. Among Virginia's best-loved military heroes were General Turner Ashby (4); Colonel John Singleton Mosby (5); General George E. Pickett (6), who led a brave but suicidal southern charge at Gettysburg; and the dashing cavalry commander, General James Ewell Brown ("Jeb") Stuart (7), who came to rival even the great Lee and Jackson in the hearts of Virginians.

1

2

3

4

5

6

7

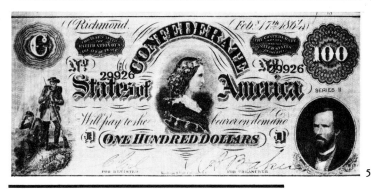

Although the Confederacy fared poorly, morale in Richmond remained high. President and Mrs. Davis were occasionally seen at parties and receptions (1), such as the one depicted opposite. Richmond's famous Tredegar Iron Works (2) produced armaments for the Confederate troops; the battery shown at upper left (3) may have been made there. Still, despite the best efforts of the workers, the Confederate troops were often woefully short of arms. Inflation became a serious problem. Bonds (4) were increasingly issued by the Confederate government to finance the war as commodities grew scarcer and prices soared. Confederate money (5) became less valuable. Inflation was evident in the rise of rates announced by the Medical College of Virginia hospital in a notice published in October 1863 (6). One reason for the rise in rates was that medical supplies, also needed by wounded soldiers, now cost more.

1

3

2

Railroads and canals were hotly contested in the war. Confederates barged war matériel (1) on the James River Canal between Lynchburg and Richmond. To prevent federal reinforcement on the Potomac, the Confederates based in Virginia destroyed the Chesapeake and Ohio Canal (2). To destroy Valley of Virginia food production, Union General Philip Sheridan ravaged the area in 1864 (3), hoping to hasten the war's end. Cadets of Virginia Military Institute helped oppose the Union army at New Market; one of ten teen-age cadets to die was Thomas Garland Jefferson (4), kinsman of the late president. In northern Virginia and the Valley, lightning attacks on federal supply trains were frequently led by Colonel John S. Mosby, shown here (5) with his mounted guerrillas destroying a Union wagon file.

4

5

In the Valley

In the autumn of 1864, after the Confederate armies had crossed into Maryland to threaten Washington and had then been pushed back, the federals increased their concentration of troops in the Shenandoah Valley, the base from which the Confederates had mounted their invasion. General Sheridan's great efforts to destroy the Valley's abundant food supplies were effective. His troops defeated a weaker Confederate force at Winchester on September 19. Bands of roaming Union and Confederate cavalry frequently clashed with each other. One such battle on the outskirts of a prosperous Valley village is shown at right (1). An important battle was fought at Cedar Creek (2) in the middle of October. At first, with Sheridan away from the field in Washington, the Confederate troops were successful. But before the battle was over, Sheridan had ridden to join his troops, rally them, and turn back the Confederate attack.

1

2

A strong defense was thrown around Washington by federal forces. Near Alexandria Unionists are shown searching a farmer's wagon (1). U.S. Army engineers built a rail bridge (2) over Potomac Creek to replace one destroyed by Confederates. Encamped at Culpeper in 1864 was General George Meade (3), who preceded Grant as commander of the Union's Army of the Potomac. A "freedmen's village" which grew at Arlington (4) drew thousands of black families who left plantations after emancipation and poured into such Unionist "slab towns" to be given food and assigned work. As Union troops gained ground in eastern Virginia, they built forts on the Potomac to prevent Confederate gunboats from reaching the District of Columbia. Above the ramparts of one such fort (5) can be seen several federal gunboats, standing guard.

3

4

5

Grant Pursues Lee

1

2

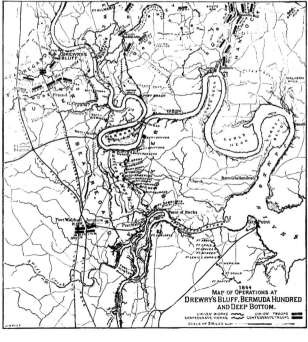

3

4

When Ulysses S. Grant (1) succeeded Meade as
Union commander at Culpeper in 1864, he began
to pursue Lee into southern Virginia. Grant, shown
on horseback (2), encamped in April 1864 at
Willcox Landing, on the north shore of the
James River in Charles City County. As Lee
moved south to Petersburg, federal gunboats (3)
moved up the James to Drewry's Bluff. A Civil
War map (4) shows Grant's pursuit of Lee south
of the James River. A significant federal engineering feat around this time was the cutting of a
canal (5) through Dutch Gap in Chesterfield
County, easing the movement of federal gunboats
up the James and expediting General Ben Butler's
operations against the Confederates. The Dutch
Gap Canal shortened the James River by five
miles. Federal control over Virginia's waterways
(6) gradually increased.

6

On the James

Once in command of federal forces in 1864, General Grant wasted no time in an effort to capture Richmond and Petersburg. A Union command post alongside the James River in 1864 (1) shows Union gunboats in control of the river and of the river steamers that traveled along it (2). General Benjamin Butler's headquarters before the siege of Petersburg were at Dutch Gap (3), in Chesterfield County. Defending the James against federal gunboats in 1864 was Howlett's Confederate battery (4). Grant's well-equipped supply depot at City Point is shown at right (5), with stacks of cannonballs in the foreground.

4

5

1

Grant's siege of Richmond and Petersburg in 1864–65 was the biggest operation of the war. A major feature was the battle of the Crater (1), in which federal troops undermined a salient (2), within Confederate lines, and set off a huge explosion on July 30, 1864. The Confederate "hero of the Crater" was General William Mahone (3), a Southampton County engineer who had been a railroad president. The siege continued through the winter of 1864–65, with federal troops (4) steadily firing. A deadly Union weapon was the "Petersburg Express" (5), a cannon mounted on a railway car, which could be moved against Lee's besieged forces at will. Casualties (6) on both sides were numerous. Lee gave orders to evacuate Petersburg (7) on April 2, 1865, after the Union army had for nine months nearly encircled the once prosperous city.

3

2

7

1

2

3

Mathew Brady and his daring photographers made some of the war's best pictures at Petersburg. The New York lensman set up his darkroom (1) along the Union lines there in 1864. Near Southside Railroad Depot, Brady photographed stacked arms (2) and partly ruined houses. This picture of the besieged city (3) was taken from a meadow across Appomattox River. After Lee's evacuation, Union wagons (4) entered Petersburg in April 1865; the picture was taken on West Washington Street, at the site of the present Petersburg High School. To replace ruined bridges, a pontoon causeway (5) was strung across the Appomattox by retreating Confederate forces to permit their withdrawal, after General Lee had decided his beleaguered forces could no longer hold Petersburg. As a result of Petersburg's capture, Richmond would also soon fall, and the Army of Northern Virginia would make its final desperate retreat to Appomattox Court House.

5

4

191

TO THE
Citizens of the State,
AND THE
PEOPLE of RICHMOND

THE ENEMY UNDOUBTEDLY

ARE APPROACHING THE CITY !

And may be expected at any hour, with a view to its capture, its pillage, and its destruction. The strongest considerations of self and of duty to the country,

CALL EVERY MAN TO ARMS !

A duty which none can refuse without dishonor. All persons, therefore, able to wield a musket, will immediately

Assemble upon the Public Square

Where a regiment will be found in arms, and around which all can rally, and where the requisite directions will be given for arming and equipping those who respond to this call.

☞ The Governor confidently relies that this appeal will not be made in vain.

WM. SMITH,

GOVERNOR OF VIRGINIA.

In April 1865, after a winter-long siege, Lee felt his troops could no longer hold Petersburg and Richmond. Accordingly, he sent word to Jefferson Davis in Richmond that the cities must be evacuated. On April 3, the Union army marched into Petersburg (1). In Richmond, Governor William H. Smith appealed to citizens to keep calm and asked all able-bodied men to fight the invaders (2). A Richmond view (3) looking westward along Main and Broad streets shows local troops in the foreground. As Confederates burned Richmond's supplies civilians streamed across the James River bridge to seek refuge in North Carolina; this Currier and Ives lithograph (4) is entitled "The Evacuation of Richmond . . . by the Government of the Southern Confederacy." From the James, lower Richmond appeared in ruins (5). OVERLEAF: Federal troops are shown triumphantly marching down Richmond's Main Street, with the Capitol at left.

As Virginia became U.S. Military District 1 of the federal government, occupation officers designated May 1, 1865, as "moving day" for ex-Confederate personnel and supplies (1). Ruined buildings lined Main Street and the dockside (2), many put to flames by evacuating Confederates to prevent their use by the Union army. Two widows of Confederates (3) sadly survey Richmond's desolation. Along the James stood the gaunt remains of the Richmond and Danville Railroad bridge (4), with the Virginia Arsenal behind it. Although many blacks remained with white families, others responded to freedom; a photograph shows a group of freedmen (5) on the bank of the James River Canal. Freed slaves and Unionists greeted President Lincoln when he came to Richmond after its capture (6); the ruined Capitol is at right.

3

4

5

6

197

Lee's Farewell

Hd Qrs: Army of N. Va:
10 April 1865 —

[General Orders No 9]

After four years of arduous service, marked by unsurpassed Courage & fortitude, the army of Northern Virginia has been compelled to yield to overwhelming numbers & resources.

I need not tell the brave survivors of so many hard fought battles, who have remained steadfast to the last, that I have consented to this result from no distrust of them; but feeling that valour & devotion could accomplish nothing that would compensate for the loss that must have attended the continuance of the contest; I determined to avoid the useless sacrifice of those, whose past services have endeared them to their Countrymen.

By the terms of the agreement, officers and men can return to their homes & remain until exchanged. You will take with you the satisfaction that proceeds from the Consciousness of duty faithfully performed, and I earnestly pray that a Merciful God will extend to you His blessing & protection.

With an unceasing admiration of your Constancy & devotion to your Country, & a grateful remembrance of your kind & generous Consideration for myself, I bid you all an affectionate farewell —

R E Lee Genl

4

Just before Lee's surrender, Union troops gathered at Appomattox Courthouse (1). The meeting between the two former West Point classmates, Lee and Grant, to arrange for the surrender of Lee's Army of Northern Virginia, took place at the McLean residence (2) near the courthouse. When news of Lee's surrender reached the Confederate cabinet on April 10, 1865, in Danville, the Confederacy was ended. Although a few Confederates received the news of Lee's surrender with cheers, according to the combat artist who portrayed the Confederate army at Appomattox for *Harper's Weekly* (3), Lee's farewell to his troops at Appomattox (4) brought tears to his soldiers' eyes. Lee's headquarters in Richmond had been the Franklin Street house of the Scotish-born merchant John Stewart; he was photographed there by Mathew Brady at the war's end (5).

5

1

2

3

A witness of Lee's agony was combat artist J. R. Chapin, who portrayed Lee's troops (1) laying down their arms at Appomattox in compliance with surrender terms. Grant permitted Confederates to keep their horses, which many needed for farming. Another artist, Alfred R. Waud, who made many of the war's best pictures, sketched Union General George Custer (2) receiving a flag of truce at Appomattox from a Confederate officer. Waud also portrayed Lee (3) proudly but sadly riding off after his surrender.

Reconstruction

Despite Lee's surrender, Jefferson Davis fled from Danville (1) and attempted to continue the war. But life returned to normal in Richmond. Train service to Washington resumed (2). In Virginia, federal occupation was resented; Richmond ladies are shown (3) sneering at a Union soldier. Davis was captured and imprisoned at Fort Monroe (4). Many former Confederates signed an oath of allegiance (5) to the United States and to the Wheeling Convention government in Virginia. A sketch (6) shows some of them taking the oath. With most ex-Confederates disfranchised, blacks were elected to most of the seats in the Virginia Constitutional Convention of 1867–68 (7). The new Constitution introduced universal male suffrage, a free public school system, and created state-supported colleges for blacks and agricultural students.

United States of America.

I, *John Sacrey*, of the County of *Fredericksburg*, State of *Va*, do solemnly swear that I will support, protect and defend the Constitution and Government of the United States against all enemies, whether domestic or foreign; that I will bear true faith, allegiance, and loyalty to the same, any ordinance, resolution or laws of any State, Convention, or Legislature, to the contrary notwithstanding; and further, that I will faithfully perform all the duties which may be required of me by the laws of the United States; and I take this oath freely and voluntarily, without any mental reservation or evasion whatever.

John Sacrey

Subscribed and sworn to before me, this *fourteenth* day of *June* A. D. 186*5*.

Maj. and Provost Marshal.

The above-named has *light* complexion, *brown* hair, and *blue* eyes; and is *5* feet *9½* inches high.

6

7

Reconciliation

1

2

3

Lee won the respect of North and South for his stoic acceptance of his fate. He undertook the presidency of Washington College at Lexington, where he was photographed (1) by Michael Miley. Mrs. Lee (2) was an invalid and had aged rapidly. A few business leaders met with Lee in 1869 at White Sulphur Springs to promote Reconstruction (3). The group included George Peabody of Nashville (left of Lee), W. W. Corcoran of Washington (right of Lee), and ex-Governor Henry Wise of Accomac (standing, second from right). Also gathered at White Sulphur (4) were Generals Joseph E. Johnston and Lee (next to tree), Wade Hampton of South Carolina (standing, left), and Lee's son, George Washington Custis Lee (seated, right). When Lee died on October 12, 1870, his funeral was held in Washington College Chapel (5). Later a chapel (6) was built, containing a recumbent figure of Lee by Edward Virginius Valentine. In Richmond, a heroic statue of the general (7) was unveiled before a crowd.

The Freed Slaves

The blacks' role in Reconstruction was a difficult one. Although few could read or write, they were urged by federal officials to vote and to hold office. A black nurse of the period (1) was photographed by the Richmond cameraman George Cook; she holds his son, Huestis, a photographer-to-be. Many blacks sold farm produce (2) at open-air markets; the vendors shown here were sketched by artist William Ludwell Sheppard. Registration of blacks to qualify them to vote was depicted in 1867 at Negro Foot in Hanover County (3). In 1867, when the federal government impaneled a jury in Richmond to try Jefferson Davis for treason (4), blacks were included in a jury for the first time in history. Black people annually celebrated January 1, "Liberation Day," with a parade commemorating Lincoln's 1863 Emancipation Proclamation; the photograph opposite (5) shows a store on Richmond's Main Street decked out for the celebration.

1

2

3

4

5

1

Along with the death of Lee, other tragedies struck Virginia in the hectic year of 1870. Rains flooded the James River and waters covered Main Street at Fifteenth (1), where the St. Charles Hotel stood (left) near the railway tracks (center). During an important trial in the courtroom on an upper story of the Capitol, the overloaded floor gave way, plunging spectators into the House of Delegates below (2). Crowds gathered outside (3) as the dead and wounded were brought out of the rubble.

1

2

The Revival of Richmond

3

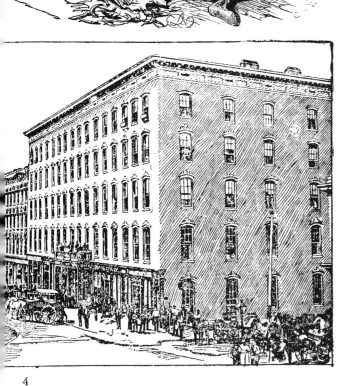

After Appomattox, the rebuilding of canals and railroads revived business life. Passengers and freight traveled by canal (1) between Richmond and Lynchburg. At Richmond, cargo could be transferred to coastal steamers bound for ports on the Atlantic coast or abroad. Canal boat life was slow, but touched with laughter and song (2). At markets, "truckers" sold produce under covered stalls (3), as depicted by William Ludwell Sheppard. A popular Richmond hotel was the Spotswood (4) on Main Street; it added to 1870's sad record of disasters when it burned that year on Christmas Day with the loss of many lives. An early Richmond practitioner of the new art of photography was George S. Cook (5), whose studio stood at 913 Main Street. He and his son, Huestis, immortalized on glass negatives many people and places of nineteenth-century Virginia.

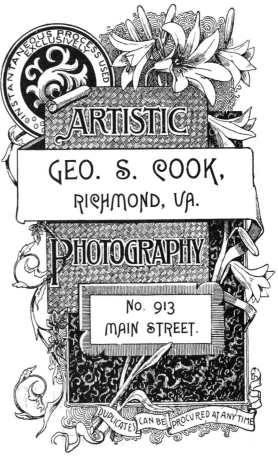

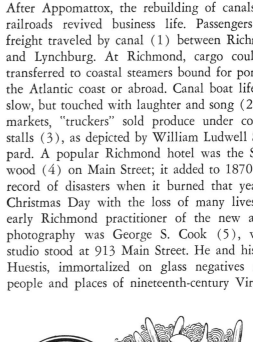

4

5

In the 1860s, the master genre painter of Virginia was William Ludwell Sheppard. Many of his earthy scenes were reproduced in *Harper's*

Weekly. His vivid depiction of the market at Richmond was printed in the issue of November 7, 1868.

1

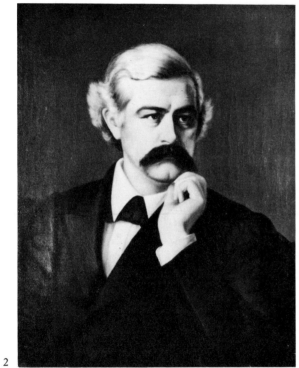

2

3

4

5

Postwar Politics

For twenty-one years after the Civil War, Richmond's Governor's Mansion (1) was in the hands of Radical Republicans and then of "Readjusters," populists who favored scaling down Virginia's debt to bondholders to benefit public schools and vocational training. In 1870, Gilbert C. Walker (2) was the first elected postwar governor. The Reverend J. E. Massey (3) was a leader of the Readjuster era, opposing Fitzhugh Lee (4), a nephew of the general, who in 1886 became the first of many conservative postwar Democratic governors. The colorful tyro of the Readjusters was ex-General William Mahone (5) of Petersburg. Fitzhugh Lee (6), at center, is shown in the picture at right with his military staff. The Readjuster Convention of 1881 (7) drew an ardent crowd, many of whom became Republicans when Mahone's power waned.

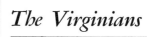

"Nowhere in America existed better human material than in the middle and lower classes in Virginia," wrote Henry Adams in the nineteenth century. Varied "Roadside Types" of the state (1) were sketched by an artist in 1874, and "Christmas in the South" (2) was limned by William Ludwell Sheppard in 1870. On the steps of Williamsburg's Nelson-Galt house in the 1890s (3), four women gathered with Prissy, a demure servinggirl; at left is Miss Emily Christian, later to be the librarian of William and Mary College. At Jonesville in Lee County, three mountaineers were photographed getting water from a public spring (4). Many venturesome Virginians went west, like Jim Bridger (5), born in Richmond in 1804 and famed at the time of his death in 1881 as a northwestern fur trader. Bridger, in 1843, founded Fort Bridger on the West's rough but romantic Oregon Trail. In 1900, a mixed Indian-Negro family (6) was photographed by James Mooney of the Bureau of American Ethnology, near the Chickahominy River; they were among the few identifiable descendants of Powhatan's once numerous people.

A New Life

1

The Christian humility of old-fashioned blacks touched the sentiment of white writers, artists, and dramatists who lived through the social chaos which followed Civil War and Emancipation. One of the most prolific artists was William Ludwell Sheppard who, in 1870, depicted a black farmwife scattering feed for her brood of chickens, while her husband set poles to support his newly planted green peas and butterbeans (1). The log shanty, chinked with mud and covered with hand-made wooden shingles, had once housed children who had grown and moved to Richmond for better pay. Equally sentimental is "A Pastoral Visit" (2), painted in 1881 by Richard N. Brooke of Warrenton, showing a family welcoming "the preacher" to its table. During decades of Negro illiteracy, black ministers offered a promise of heavenly reward to those who bore the world's sufferings with Christian faith. Black ministers sometimes gave schooling, legal advice, and even medical care.

2

1

The Religious Spirit

The church was the core of most society in Virginia until the mid-twentieth century. Outdoor mass baptisms brought throngs of converts and onlookers each summer. Huestis Cook photographed this scene (1) under a noonday sky on the shore of a Tidewater river. Another popular ritual was the camp meeting, or "protracted" meeting, when the preacher frightened his listeners with the prospect of eternal damnation unless they repented their sins and offered themselves for baptism and a Christian life. This scene showing repentant sinners (2) appeared in *Frank Leslie's Illustrated Weekly* as part of a series on black life in post-Civil War Virginia.

2

Self-Improvement

The slow rise of blacks was chiefly due to education. Nearly all were illiterate in 1870, the year when black voters registered to cast ballots in Richmond's first postwar election (1). A famed black preacher was Richmond's John Jasper (2), whose "The Sun Do Move" sermon was widely repeated. The best-known early twentieth-century black was Booker T. Washington (3), born near Rocky Mount and educated at Hampton Institute. An 1899 Hampton Institute history class (4) is shown inspecting an Indian. Carpentry and other manual skills (5) were also taught at the Institute. The Institute's chapel (6) was one of many structures built with the aid of donations and the earnings of Hampton's choir. Hampton graduates, like the man shown seated in his comfortable dining room (7), rose to middle-class status.

2

3

4

5

1

3

4

6

7

Railroads spurred travel, and scenes of America blossomed in magazines. *Scribner's Monthly* devoted much of its April 1874 issue to "A Ramble in Virginia," which described life in a state still recovering from the ravages of war. Illustrations showed Wytheville, the county seat of Wythe (1); a springs hotel in the Blue Ridge area (2); the newly important southwestern Virginia rail center of Bristol, on the Tennessee border (3); the Roanoke Valley between Lynchburg and Big Lick, soon to be renamed Roanoke (4); a side street in Lynchburg, looking uphill from a warehouse area (5); the James River at Lynchburg, spanned by one of the covered bridges of the upland region (6); a bird's-eye view of the river below Lynchburg, with a canal paralleling the river (7); and Lynchburg's outdoor market, with housewives eyeing the wares of produce sellers seated among the cobblestones (8).

8

Virginia Scenery

Nineteenth-century Virginia offered few man-made wonders, but sightseers admired its romantic landscape. In his *Picturesque America,* Henry Linton showed a view atop Natural Bridge (1), with its cascading stream below. In the same book appeared a drawing of Cumberland Gap (2), with the rocky Wilderness Road blazed in 1775 by Daniel Boone visible intermittently as it moved westward to Kentucky. The Dismal Swamp, which captured the imagination of Poe and others with its legends of man-killing bears, lost huntsmen, and unfathomed mysteries, attracted many visitors. This view (3) of the locks and keeper's house along the Dismal Swamp Canal, from Norfolk southward into North Carolina, was made in 1873. Nowhere was the melancholy of change more evident than at Jamestown, which had all but disappeared until the Association for the Preservation of Virginia Antiquities took over part of it in the 1890s. A painting by T. B. Schell (4) shows the ruined tower of the 1639 brick church standing close to the rapidly eroding shoreline.

3

4

The Yorktown Centennial

Virginia was too poor to take part in the 1876 World's Fair in Philadelphia, but Yorktown was the scene of a great three-day blast in 1881, on the one hundredth anniversary of Cornwallis's surrender. President Chester Arthur laid the cornerstone of the Victory Monument on October 19 (1). A navy flotilla brought many Washington VIPs down to Yorktown, and excursion boats (2) conveyed others. A photograph of the period shows a naval vessel at Yorktown (3). The U.S. Marine Band, led by twenty-seven-year-old John Philip Sousa (4), played for the three-day ceremonies, which were attended by twenty thousand. To amuse guests, a temporary theater, the first in the dusty village of Yorktown, offered plays nightly (5).

4

5

1

2

3

4

5

6

The state's first land-grant school, later Virginia Polytechnic Institute and State University, was founded at Blacksburg in 1872 (1). Around the same time, the Grammar and Matty School was founded in Williamsburg. A 1910 photograph (2) shows its students gathered at the tomb of little Matthew Whaley in Bruton Churchyard. In 1865, Virginia Military Institute's leaders (3) were urged by Superintendent Francis Smith (standing) to revive the school. Present were ex-Governor Letcher (third from left, seated) and Matthew Fontaine Maury (seventh from left, seated). The Reverend William Henry Ruffner (4) of Rockbridge became Virginia's first public school head in 1870. A pioneer black educator was Maggie L. Walker (5) of Richmond. General Samuel Armstrong (6) of Connecticut founded a freedmen's school, which became Hampton Institute. The College of William and Mary was revived in 1888, after a seven-year lapse, with a faculty of "Seven Wise Men" (7).

Standing: Prof. Hugh Bird, Dr. T. J. Stubbs, Dr. C. Bishop

7

1

2

Although Richmond and Norfolk became commercial hubs, once proud Williamsburg long remained an unpaved county seat. From the cupola of the Wren Building, an 1859 cameraman looked down Duke of Gloucester Street on a snowy day (1). Oxcarts were still used in 1918, as this photograph shows (2). It was taken in front of the unrestored printing office, then a store, on Duke of Gloucester Street. The Lunatic Asylum (3) was America's first public mental institution when built in 1773, but its main building was burned in the nineteenth century. Duke of Gloucester Street (4) remained unpaved until World War I; this picture was taken about 1890 from College Corner. On the same street, near the site of the destroyed Capitol, was the S. Harris Cheap Store (5), whose front had been added to a colonial structure.

3

4

5

1

A MERRY CHRISTMAS TO ALL

The Spotswood Hotel

BILL OF FARE

Christmas, 1870

Soup

Mock Turtle   Mulligatawney

Fish

Boiled Chub, Shrimp Sauce Trout a la Royal

Turkey, Oyster Sauce
Leg of Valley Mutton, Caper Sauce
Chine and Turnips   Bacon and Greens
Corned Beef
Westphalia Ham and Cabbage
Capons, Egg Sauce

Cold Dishes

Boned Turkey, Aspic Jelly Westphalia Ham
Hog's Head Cheese   Beef Tongue, Veal
Pressed Corned Beef   Roast Beef
Valley Mutton   Turkey

Salads

Chicken Cole Slaw Celery, Lobster

Entrees

Fillet de Boeuf aux Champignons
Scallop of Sweetbreads a la Marechal
Vol-a-Vent of Cherrystone Oysters
Calf's Head a la Tartare
Queen Fritters, Vanilla Flavor
Fricandeau de Veau Aux Petits Pois
Epigramme of Venison, Bread Sauce
Curry of Chicken a la Indienne
Timbale of Macaroni a la Milanese
Partridges a la Maitre d'Hotel

Roast

Turkey, Giblet Sauce   Ribs of Beef
Saddle of South Down Mutton
Fig Stuffed
Goose Apple Sauce, Loin of Veal
Westphalia Ham, Champagne Sauce

Sprigtail Duck
Saddle of Venison, Currant Jelly
Blackhead Duck

Relishes

Pickled Cucumbers   Tomato Catsup
Sweet Damson Pickles
Worcestershire Sauce   Walnut Catsup
Horse Radish
Mixed Pickles   French Mustard
Pickled Cherries   English Mustard
Cranberry Jelly   Spanish Olives

Vegetables

Boiled Potatoes   Baked Potatoes
Onions   Turnips
Salsify   Cabbage
Mashed Potatoes   Sweet Potatoes
Parsnips   Spinach
Stewed Potatoes   Rice
Rice Hominy

Pastry

English Plum Pudding, Brandy Sauce
Mince Pie
Fruit Cake Pound Cake Sponge Cake
Lady Fingers   Tartlet Meringues
Coconut Custard Pies   Apple Pies
Spanish Macaroons

Dessert

Apples Almonds Pecan Nuts Filberts
Lemon Ice Cream   Madeira Jelly

Coffee

To its farm produce, Virginia added the gustatory treats of Chesapeake Bay. The bill of fare of Richmond's Spotswood Hotel (1) lists dishes for Christmas Day, 1870—when the hotel accidentally burned. Shad were abundant each spring; a view (2) on the James, below the fall line, shows farm hands hauling in a shad net. Beginning in September, the oyster-dredging season produced millions of shellfish; at shucking houses (3), blacks stood all day with knives, opening bivalves for customers. The choicest gourmet specialty was the diamondback terrapin; an 1889 magazine illustration (4) shows how terrapin were caught. During the winter's first big freeze—usually in January—farmers killed hogs, hanging their carcasses to drain before cutting and salting, as this black family is shown doing in 1900 (5). At rail stops, vendors sold home-cooked delicacies to passengers. At Gordonsville, on the C & O, the "local commissary department" serves customers (6).

The Railroads

1

The railroad dominated the boom-and-bust economy which followed the Civil War and Reconstruction. The Richmond Locomotive and Machine Works was a major Virginia industry whose workers (1) made many steam locomotives to haul coal from mines in southwest Virginia and Kentucky. An advertisement for the company appeared in Chataigne's Directory of Richmond in 1888 (2). The largest line to serve Virginia was the Chesapeake and Ohio. The C & O station at Wickham (3), in Hanover County, was named for General Williams Carter Wickham, CSA, an early president of the line. An 1875 timetable (4) of a Virginia road showed a typical engine, coal car, freight car, and passenger carriage. The Italianate C & O depot in Richmond (5) was abandoned in the 1970s, after passenger service succumbed to the automobile and the airplane.

2

3

TIME TABLE

NO. 2,

Atlantic, Miss. & Ohio R. R.

NORFOLK & PETERSBURG AND SOUTH SIDE DIVISIONS,

TO GO INTO EFFECT

SUNDAY, NOV'R 28th, 1875,

AT 5:20 A. M.

PETERSBURG:
FROM JOHN B. EGE'S JOB PRINTING HOUSE.
1875.

4

5

237

Growing and Curing Tobacco

"The black belt," south of the James, was a world unto itself. There the all-consuming interest was tobacco (1), which grew richly in Southside counties. After being cut in late summer, the leaf was hung up to "cure" in crude "barns" (2), strung up on long lathes (3) to dry before being taken to the nearest auction for sale to the highest bidder. Inside early tobacco factories, black workers (4) deftly cut the rough stems from tobacco leaves. Women and children (5) labored long hours stemming and packing tobacco, to be made into cigarettes or shipped to Europe, where "Virginia tobacco" retained the fame it had acquired in John Rolfe's time at Jamestown, when the first crops were shipped.

The Tobacco Market

1

2

The growing and selling of tobacco was a ritual performed each summer in southern Virginia. At Drake's Branch in about 1900, a photographer shot this collection of farm wagons (1), bringing leaf to a warehouse for sale. A horn blast (2) summoned buyers and sellers to the opening at auction houses. Although it stood on the fringe of tobaccoland, Richmond long remained its capital; the Tobacco Exchange (3) stood at the corner of Cary and Virginia streets, accessible to the canal which brought shipments down the James. Contesting with Richmond for primacy in tobacco wealth were Lynchburg and Danville; on the Dan River at Danville (4) stood several major leaf warehouses. A postwar Virginia manufacturer of tobacco was the Richmond firm of Allen and Ginter, whose Richmond Straight Cut No. 1 cigarettes (5) were widely advertised. Major Lewis Ginter became one of Richmond's earliest industrial millionaires and developed Ginter Park.

3

4

A Group of Warehouses.

The Richmond Straight Cut No. 1
CIGARETTES

Are made from the brightest, most delicately flavored and highest cost **Gold Leaf** grown in Virginia. This is the **Old and Original brand** of **Straight Cut Cigarettes**, and was brought out by us in the year 1875

BEWARE OF IMITATIONS, and observe that the *firm name as below* is on every package.

ALLEN & GINTER, Manuf's.

Richmond, Virginia;

THE LIBRARY.

"QUITTING

The advent of the cigarette as the favorite American smoke created new wealth in a few southern Virginia cities. Three scenes from a cigarette factory, sketched by John Durkin, appeared in *Harper's Weekly* in January 1887 (1); rolling and cutting, at first done by hand, were later automatized. Although whites were hired for finishing jobs, blacks continued to predominate in other phases of tobacco production, as in this sorting and stemming room (2). By 1905, Richmond's prosperous Main Street showed no signs of Civil War damage, but flaunted its tobacco prosperity in banners for locally manufactured cigarettes (3). Many of the Victorian storefronts shown in the photograph are still in evidence today.

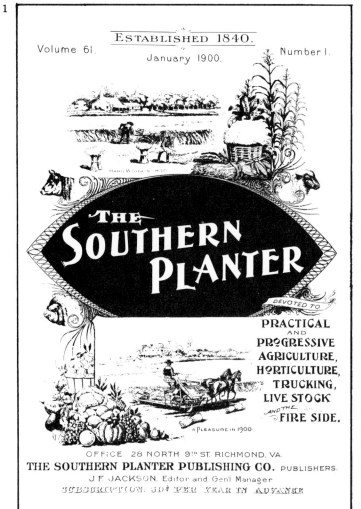

A leading voice in agricultural matters for decades was Richmond's *Southern Planter* (1), a magazine begun in 1840. Most small farms raised a few pigs, killing them each winter (2) and hanging the carcasses before cutting the meat and curing some of it for the warm months. Cotton was widely grown in southern Virginia (3) after Eli Whitney invented the cotton gin in 1793, but the crop moved south in the twentieth century. Peanuts became a big crop south of the James in the Civil War era, with markets developing at Petersburg, Smithfield, Suffolk, and elsewhere; an advertisement in Edward Pollock's *Historical and Industrial Guide to Petersburg* in 1884 offered packaging and marketing services to growers (4). On farms, bullocks hauled wagons (5) and plows; although slower than horses and mules, they were stronger and more patient.

OVERLEAF: Tenants on a Southside farm are seen picking peanuts by hand.

The big Sussex County plantation, Tower Hill,
owned by the Blow family, was drawn by Major
William Blow about 1900. The mansion itself is

labeled A; "offices" and workshops B to P; barns
and stables Q to X; and servants' quarters Y
and Z.

The First Families

Family life was close in horse-and-buggy days. Frances Booth was photographed sitting on her Carter's Grove porch about 1890 (1). On the Pagan River at Smithfield, the Frank Berrymans built a Victorian house (2) with gazebo, boathouse, and a conveniently moored yacht, the *Jean and Virginia*. At Tuckahoe in Goochland, Major and Mrs. Richard Allen and their son (3) posed for Huestis Cook. The family of Major Augustus Drewry (4) was similarly depicted at Westover, with the James in the background. Family mementos fill the parlor of Miss Elizabeth Beverley Coleman, right (5), at Williamsburg in 1902. The daughter of Dr. Charles Washington Coleman, she was a descendant of the Tuckers and a sister of George Preston Coleman, mayor of Williamsburg and first state highway head in Virginia. Above the mantel clock in the parlor hangs the popular print, "The Burial of Latane."

Many great houses fell victim to Virginia's declining nineteenth-century prosperity. One was Rosewell, on the York in Gloucester County, which

was photographed in the early twentieth-century,
before its walls collapsed. Built by John Page, it
often housed Jefferson and other great figures.

3

Horseflesh attracted Virginians from early days. Many champions were bred to race and win meets throughout the eastern states. Diomed (1) was a famous Virginia thoroughbred who won many nineteenth-century North-South races. Sir Archy (2) was a fast starter in quarter-mile races and progenitor of noted quarter horses. Fox hunting was a favorite pursuit from George Washington's time; George S. Cook took this picture about 1900 (3). Jumping Virginia's split-rail fences tested the mettle of mount and rider; a Huestis Cook photograph (4) dates from a time when most women still rode sidesaddle. A survival of medieval England was the jousting tournament (5), in which riders sought to impale suspended rings on their lances while riding at breakneck speed. By World War II, such rural pursuits had largely disappeared.

4

5

256

Society

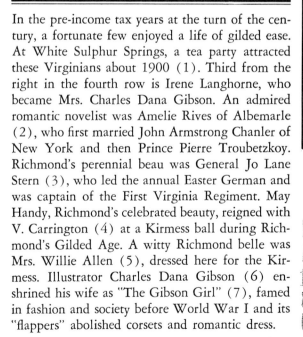

In the pre-income tax years at the turn of the century, a fortunate few enjoyed a life of gilded ease. At White Sulphur Springs, a tea party attracted these Virginians about 1900 (1). Third from the right in the fourth row is Irene Langhorne, who became Mrs. Charles Dana Gibson. An admired romantic novelist was Amelie Rives of Albemarle (2), who first married John Armstrong Chanler of New York and then Prince Pierre Troubetzkoy. Richmond's perennial beau was General Jo Lane Stern (3), who led the annual Easter German and was captain of the First Virginia Regiment. May Handy, Richmond's celebrated beauty, reigned with V. Carrington (4) at a Kirmess ball during Richmond's Gilded Age. A witty Richmond belle was Mrs. Willie Allen (5), dressed here for the Kirmess. Illustrator Charles Dana Gibson (6) enshrined his wife as "The Gibson Girl" (7), famed in fashion and society before World War I and its "flappers" abolished corsets and romantic dress.

7

Getting Together

4

Conviviality was part of Virginia life. A mandolin club (1) gathered in Wetherburn's Tavern yard in Williamsburg about 1900, led by Miss Pinky Morecock, seated at left. Young Richmonders formed a handsome Greek chorus (2) in an 1896 theatrical. Ministers of the Potomac Baptist Association (3) gathered in northern Virginia in 1897, dressed in the somber habiliments of their calling. The 1875 graduating class at Hampton Institute (4) posed with President Samuel Armstrong, who stands second from left in the third row. At Washington and Lee University, the Troubadours in 1898 presented *Hamlet* (5), with Ophelia at left and the gloomy Dane at right.

5

1

2

3

4

5

Preserving the Past

The saving of Virginia's historic sites gained momentum in 1888 when two ladies bought Williamsburg's Powder Magazine (1) and the next year began the Association for the Preservation of Virginia Antiquities. They were Miss Mary Galt of Norfolk (2) and Mrs. Charles Washington Coleman of Williamsburg (3). Also a leader was Lyon Gardiner Tyler (4), president of the revived College of William and Mary. In 1903, Bruton Parish Church called the Reverend W. A. R. Goodwin (5), and he intensified the movement. To the APVA, the state of Virginia deeded Jamestown's ruined church (6), then endangered by erosion and souvenir hunters. Interest in Jamestown grew in 1898, after Ambler descendants gathered in the ruins of their burned plantation house on Jamestown Island (7); soon thereafter, it was bought by the National Park Service.

1

2

A Last Hurrah for the Confederacy

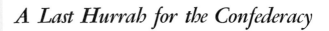

Many Confederate reunions were held in Richmond before the last of the veterans died in the mid-twentieth century. In 1907, the unveiling of an equestrian statue of General Jeb Stuart drew nearly ten thousand parading old soldiers from the South (1). The Richmond Blues strutted smartly down Franklin Street, approaching the statue. At the base of the nearby Lee monument (2), children formed a Confederate flag. Stonewall Jackson's horse, Little Sorrel (3), was kept proudly for years at Virginia Military Institute until its death. Below, a dignified group of Richmond ladies, along with an escort, are shown celebrating Confederate Memorial Day (4).

1

2

Virginia's Seaports

3

An International Naval Rendezvous (1) took place in Hampton Roads in 1893, on the four hundredth anniversary of Columbus's arrival in the New World; it featured reconstructions of Columbus's ships and warships of the world's navies. Norfolk's harbor (2) was the maritime center of Virginia. (At left is the port's domed courthouse, at center the customs house.) Goliath of Virginia transport in the 1880s was Collis Huntington (3), standing at left with a newsboy and a nephew. Huntington built Newport News as the C & O's terminus and put a shipyard there. Drydock 1 (4) was opened in 1889. In 1906, schooners (5) were still being repaired at the yard.

4

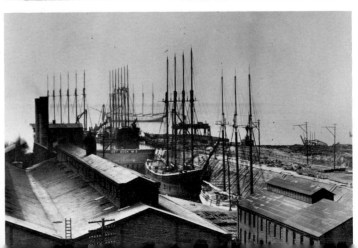

5

The Unspoiled Countryside

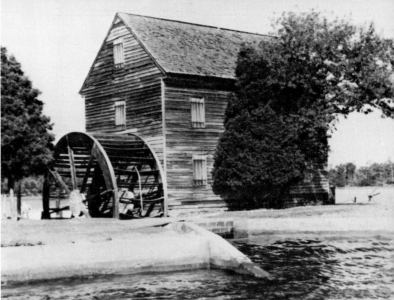

Old ways lingered on in an industrial age. Over Walker Creek in Giles County, a swinging bridge (1) offered excitement to all but the fainthearted. In rural Mathews County, pierced by dozens of tidal creeks, this tide mill (2) operated until late in the nineteenth century, grinding corn into meal and wheat into flour. Elsewhere in Virginia, water-mills continued to operate well into this century, chiefly in central and upland Virginia, where wheat grew more abundantly and labor was cheaper. At Thumb Run in Fauquier County, Sunday church-goers gathered outside the Baptist church after the service (3), as Americans had been doing for centuries.

1

2

Many early photographs of Virginia life were the work of Frances Benjamin Johnston, who traveled around the state taking pictures of a changing era. At a fair in May 1903, she set up a booth to take tintypes; another photographer photographed her, standing at center (1). The life of blacks attracted Miss Johnston's sympathies; she photographed this cabin (2) made of rough siding and shingles, with a chimney of mud and scantling, similar to the wattle-and-daub chimneys built by Jamestown's earliest settlers. Children dressed for Sunday School (3) were photographed in another rural setting.

268

3

When the Spanish-American War broke out in 1898, the ebullient Fitzhugh Lee (1), ex-governor and kinsman of Robert E. Lee, was American consul general in Cuba. He returned to Washington as a hero and was made a major general. The Newport News–built gunboat U.S.S. *Nashville* (2) fired the first shot in the war on April 22, 1898. Norfolk and Newport News became important ports of embarkation; troops encamped by the James River, alongside the Newport News Shipbuilding and Dry Dock Company, awaiting navy transports to take them into combat (3). In Richmond, the Light Infantry Blues were photographed (4) marching down Cary Street, past Seventh Street, on their way to Byrd Street Depot to board a train for Jacksonville and embarkation. Wrote Asbury Christian: "Crowds stood on the streets and cheered them. . . . Wives, mothers, sisters, and sweethearts were left behind weeping."

4

A New Era

Technology rapidly transformed the shape of life in post-Civil War Virginia. Richmond's 1881 telephone switchboard (1) was shaped like a pyramid and operated by young ladies in full skirts. Although the horse and carriage (2) still provided fast transport along Richmond streets, at a time when other cities still used horse-drawn street cars Richmond in the 1880s had electric trolleys (3); it claimed to have the first all-electric system in the nation. Richmond's Broad Street in 1913 (4) still had few motorists, for most people traveled downtown by trolley car. Another view of Broad Street about the same time (5) reveals three early automobiles, parked not far from the Bijou Theatre, of fond memory. On the corner at left stood the Colonial Theatre, price 10¢. Little changed except for its two wings added in 1904 was Virginia's Capitol (6).

1

2

3

4

5

6

Art and Science

1

2

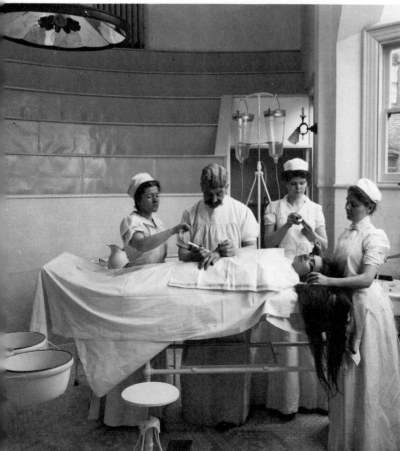

3

Art and science attracted many careerists in the twentieth century. The original Egyptian Building (1) of Richmond's Medical College of Virginia, founded in 1837, was crowded with students after merging in 1913 with University College of Medicine. Shown operating at Virginia Hospital in Richmond about 1902 is Dr. Jacob Michaux (2), photographed by Edythe Beveridge. Dr. Walter Reed (3), born in Gloucester, conquered yellow fever as a result of army medical research in Cuba. Prominent sculptor and founder of Richmond's Valentine Museum was Edward Virginius Valentine (4), shown in his studio; serving as a model for Valentine's statue of Robert E. Lee in Washington's Capitol was Robert E. Lee, Jr. (5), seen posing in his underwear. The favorite haunt of distinguished Richmond residents was the Westmoreland Club (6) at Sixth and Grace streets. It later merged with the Commonwealth Club and was replaced by another structure.

6

1

Richmond Life

With each war, more rural Virginians became familiar with the pleasures of city life—and stayed in town. The Spanish-American War brought people to Virginia's cities, as the Revolution and Civil War had done. A popular Richmond figure of the nineties was the organ grinder, shown in a picture (1) taken about 1890. A ghostly presence on Broad Street was Swan Tavern (2), once a celebrated hotel but by the 1890s a ruin. Pursued by children in summer was the ice wagon (3), photographed about 1898 on North Sixth Street in Richmond, alongside the Second Market. In that pre-Prohibition age, saloons flourished. In Richmond's Commerce Cafe (4), which stood on the north side of Main Street, between Ninth and Tenth streets, spirits flowed briskly. At the Sixth Street Market in Richmond (5), carts from nearby counties offered country produce. The Richmond German celebrated Easter in 1890 with its traditional Monday dance (6).

3

4

5

6

Virginia's Birthday

For the three hundredth anniversary of Virginia's settlement in 1907, Virginia built the Jamestown Exposition at Pine Beach, near Norfolk. Though beset by debt and delay, the exposition attracted exhibits from foreign governments and from the thirteen original states. Warships of many nations gathered in Hampton Roads on May 13, 1907, to mark the anniversary of the first permanent English settlement in North America. From Washington, President Theodore Roosevelt came to Norfolk aboard a naval yacht. Shown projecting from the shoreline at left is the Exposition's International Lagoon, in which historic and colorful ships were berthed. The navy had taken over the site by World War I for its Atlantic fleet.

The Lure of the Water

1

2

3

Surf bathing was uncommon in the puritanical nineteenth century, but it bloomed in the twentieth. By 1913, Virginia Beach (1) had become popular with both bathers and boardwalkers. Nearby, at Ocean View, the wide white beach (2) attracted many vacationers. The Virginia Boat Club raced eight-oared craft in the James River at Richmond each summer. Here (3) a crew in the 1920s prepares to embark from its dock on Mayo's Island, with the ancient form of Dunlop's flour mill in the background. A familiar sight along coastal waterways until World War II were river steamers, like the S.S. *Hampton Roads* (4) of the Old Dominion Line, which operated daily except Sunday between Norfolk, Newport News, and Smithfield. The growth of automobile traffic and the spread of bridges and tunnels after the 1920s doomed the steamboats.

4

1

2

3

"The law" seemed ominous to the young, the poor, and the naïve. The courtroom was awesome (1), even though the judge and jurors might sit in shirt-sleeves in hot weather. During the Prohibition era, the making of corn whiskey (2) flourished at bootleg distilleries hidden in Virginia's woods and mountains. Lynching, or "Lynch law"(3), occasionally was visited by mobs on suspected murderers or rapists. However, a strong antilynching law was adopted under Governor Harry Byrd, bringing an end to the practice. Virginia's anti-lynch law was later copied by other states.

1

2

On The Road

A revolution in life swept Virginia after World War I. In those years the automobile displaced the horse, resulting in swifter movement, better schools, bigger cities, and an endless spread of hard-surfaced roads. In the waning years of the horse, these photos were taken on Virginia roads. A wagon bus for school children (1) operated in one upland Virginia county. At the Edinburg post

3

4

office, in upland Virginia, Frank Jennings loads his mail wagon (2). One of the last covered bridges in western Virginia (3) was over the north fork of the Shenandoah River. A buggy (4) is shown approaching a wooden bridge over North Mayo River. Even after automobiles became common, mules frequently had to drag them out of the mud, as illustrated in this view (5) of a Model T Ford being rescued in 1917 near Dumfries, on the road that was later to be hard-surfaced as U.S. Highway 1.

5

1

2

3

4

Of all her sons, Virginia admires statesmen and military leaders most. George C. Marshall was born in Pennsylvania, but he graduated in 1901 from Virginia Military Institute. In the photograph opposite (1) he is shown seated third from left, wearing the insignia as first captain of cadets. The next year Marshall (again third from left) married Elizabeth Carter Coles of Lexington, seen standing next to him (2). They are shown posing with members of the bridal party and their parents on the Coles' porch. Shown at left (3) with friends at the University of Virginia is Woodrow Wilson. Wilson's birthplace, the Presbyterian manse in Staunton (4), is preserved today as it then was, with the Pierce-Arrow he used as president in front. In 1912, Wilson returned to his birthplace (5), a few months before his inauguration as president, accompanied by Virginia's white-bearded Governor William Hodges Mann. Wilson's birthplace is kept open to the public by the Woodrow Wilson Foundation at Staunton, while the George C. Marshall Museum and Library have been built on the grounds of Virginia Military Institute at Lexington.

5

World War I

During World War I, strategic Hampton Roads became an area of military and naval concentration, to remain so thereafter. At Mulberry Island on the lower James, the army built Fort Eustis (1), now headquarters of the Army Transportation Command. At Newport News, the army in 1917 built Camp Stuart (2) to receive troops for transport overseas. To speed the construction of navy convoy vessels, the Newport News shipyard on July 4, 1918, held "Liberty Launching Day" (3) to launch three destroyers in succession. At the new Naval Air Station at Norfolk (4) a flyer prepared to climb into the gondola of a navy observation blimp. Women volunteers trimmed a Christmas tree (5) in 1918 for soldiers in U.S. Debarkation Hospital 51 at Hampton. The flyers at the Norfolk Naval Air Station were by no means the first Virginians to take to the air. Almost a decade before World War I, the Wright brothers' plane was flown for tests at Fort Myer, in northern Virginia (6).

4

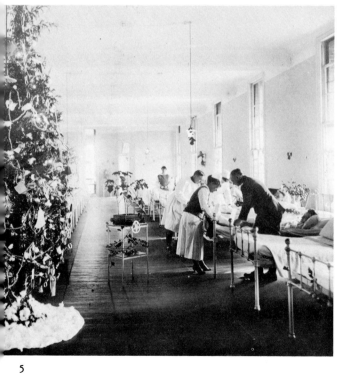

5

6

Disasters

Two tragedies that became part of America's consciousness occurred early in the twentieth century in Virginia. At Danville on September 27, 1903, a fast mail train hurtled from a trestle and killed its crewmen, leaving a shattered wreck (1,2). The incident inspired the folk song "The Wreck of Old 97." The Italian dirigible *Roma* (3) came to Langley Field, at Hampton, in 1921 for Army Air Corps trials. Three months later, she crashed and burned at Norfolk, killing thirty-four men. A public memorial service (4) was held at the Casino grounds in Newport News. The U.S. Post Office flag flies at half-staff in the background.

1

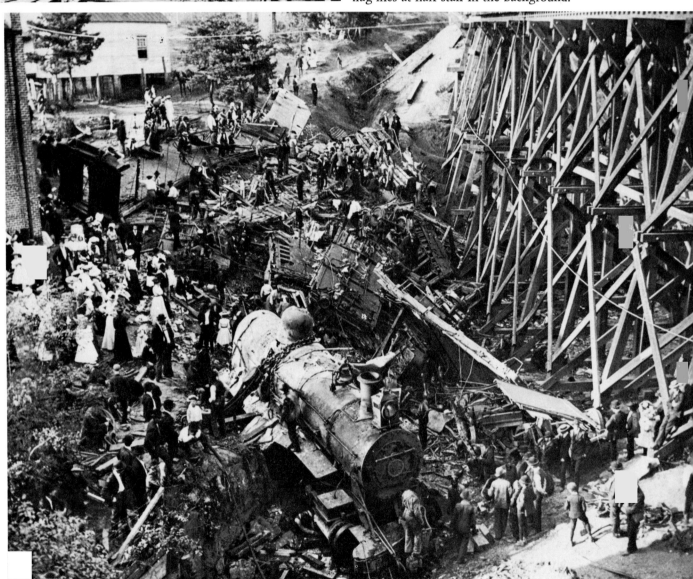

2

3

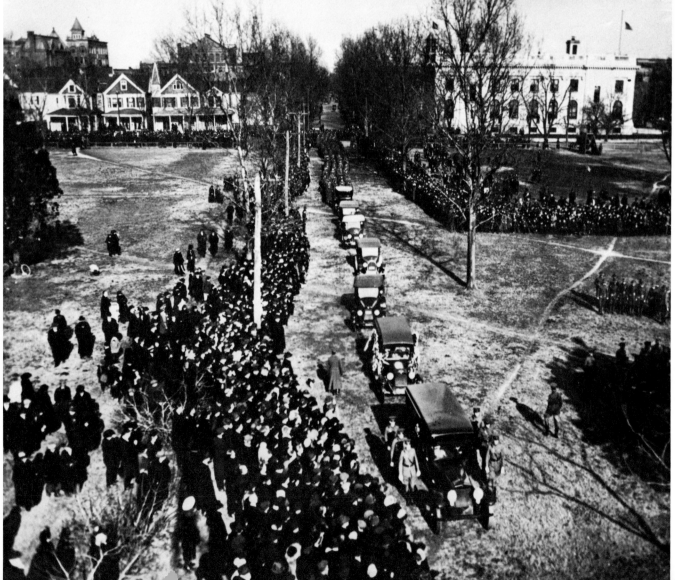

4

1

2

In the chivalric tradition of the South, Virginia was slow to give women the vote. The Equal Suffrage League of Richmond appeared outside the State Capitol in 1916 to demand the vote (1). On the Capitol steps (2), the league plumped for the Nineteenth Amendment. However, the Assembly demurred until Congress adopted the measure in 1919. A Virginia-born spokeswoman for the cause was Nancy Langhorne, who became Lady Astor and returned in 1922 to Danville, her early home. A crowd gathered to see her at the house which had served briefly in 1865 as the last Confederate headquarters (3). Lady Astor received this cup (4) as a tribute from the citizens of Danville. The "flapper era" was in full swing in the 1920s (5), when two jubilant young ladies crossed the brand-new James River Bridge, a five-mile structure linking Newport News with Isle of Wight County and southern Virginia.

1

2

3

6

7

Halls of Learning

The era of the two world wars stimulated higher education—and changed it radically. Virginia's first coeds were admitted to William and Mary in 1918 (1), introducing aesthetic dancing to unbelieving male students. Relatively unchanged were two other early schools, both in Lexington: Washington and Lee University (2), and Virginia Military Institute (3), begun as an arsenal in 1839. Some educators exerted wide influence. At William and Mary, Julian Alvin Carrol Chandler (4) revolutionized the college in a fifteen-year span. In 1904, Edwin A. Alderman (5) became the first president in the history of the University of Virginia. Francis Pendleton Gaines (6) headed Washington and Lee, and Frederic W. Boatwright (7) led the University of Richmond for fifty-one years. At William and Mary in 1926, President Coolidge and Governor Harry Byrd received honorary degrees (8).

8

1

2

A Tradition of the Arts

3

Virginia's writers lingered long in the romantic tradition. Mary Johnston (1) of Richmond and Warm Springs wrote turn-of-the-century historical novels. Poet Abram Joseph Ryan (2) dwelt lovingly on the Confederacy. John Fox, Jr. (3), of Big Stone Gap, created such best sellers as *The Trail of the Lonesome Pine* and married musical-comedy star Fritzi Scheff. Willa Cather (4), born near Winchester of Germanic parents, moved west at the age of nine. Pearl Buck (5), daughter of missionaries to China, graduated from Randolph-Macon Woman's College in 1914. Sherwood Anderson (6) came to Marion, Virginia, in mid-career and published its newspaper while continuing to write. John Powell (7) wrote of Appalachian musical sources but was famed chiefly as a composer and pianist. A collation at the Richmond home (8) of Ellen Glasgow, second from left, attracted literati.

296

4

5

6

7

8

1

The Byrds and Their Opponents

After Reconstruction, Democrats dominated the state. Competition was often keen between Organization and non-Organization Democrats. In 1919, Indians (1) gave a traditional Thanksgiving gift to Governor Westmoreland Davis, a non-Organization man. Carter Glass (2), a Lynchburg newspaperman, became a non-Organization leader and was named to the Senate by Davis in 1921. Glass was greeted in Washington by Vice President Marshall and Senator Underwood of Alabama

3

2

4

5

(3); Glass is at the left. Other non-Organization leaders were John Randolph Tucker (4) and his son, Harry St. George Tucker (5), who both represented the Lexington district. But Virginia's top political family was the Byrds. The flyer, Richard E. Byrd was given a ticker-tape parade in New York in 1930 (6) after his polar expedition. His brother, Harry Byrd (second from left), was photographed (7) after his 1926 inauguration as governor, together with his son, Harry, Jr., later a U.S. Senator, and his father, Richard E. Byrd, ex-Speaker of the House of Delegates.

1

2

The automobile age revolutionized America, but rural Virginia was slow to respond. Country fiddlers continued to gather each year at the White Top Music Festival near Abingdon, as this group did in 1925 (1). During the Great Depression, in 1939, a farm wife, Mrs. Bailey Nicholson (2), appeared thus at her home in the uplands of Shenandoah National Park. A roadside shack (3) at Bartlett, in Southside Virginia, was plastered with signs in the 1930s, including one for a three-cent soft drink. Running water was rare in Depression-era farmhouses, as evidenced by this pump primer near Herndon, in northern Virginia (4). One harbinger of great change was the damming of southern Virginia's tempestuous Roanoke River, along the North Carolina line, in the 1930s. Bugg's Island Dam (5), in Mecklenburg County, was one of a series of impoundments that provided electric power and created freshwater lakes offering fishing, swimming, and boating. To realize the project, the federal government bought and flooded thousands of river-bottom acres in the tobacco belt.

3

5

Politicians and Their Works

In southwest Virginia, bitter fights pitted Democrats and Republicans in the "Fighting Ninth" district. A notable Republican leader was C. Bascom Slemp of Wise County (1), who held the House of Representatives seat from 1907 to 1923. He was a close friend of President and Mrs. Calvin Coolidge (2). Rapid growth in the economy followed World War I. Newport News benefited in 1922 when the captured German transport *Vaterland* was converted into the *Leviathan,* America's largest ship (3). At Big Meadows in 1936, President Franklin Roosevelt spoke at the dedication of Shenandoah National Park (4), which led campers and motorists along the crest of the mountains. Ultimately, the park was extended southwestward into North Carolina. One outdoorsman who favored the park plan was Senator Harry Byrd, Sr. (5), of Berryville, shown on an overlook near the Appalachian Trail, which he frequently followed on weekend hiking trips.

BARBECUE

For Congress

For Congress

HON. C. B. SLEMP.

Hon. C. B. Slemp, Hon. T. J. Muncy and others
WILL SPEAK AT
Pennington Gap,
SATURDAY,
OCTOBER 29
Music by Brass Band

Let Democrats, Republicans and every one come out and hear our distinguished young Congressman who is native of our great county, and who as Congressman has represented all the people regardless of politics, and his associates discuss fairly and impartially the issues of the campaign. Ladies are Especially Invited.

1

2

3

4

5

2

3

In a sectionalized post–Civil War nation, the writing of history increasingly occupied Virginians of scholarly bent. They felt a need to depict Virginia's highly significant role in the nation's history. The Virginia Historical Society (1) in 1899 moved into the wartime Richmond home of Robert E. Lee, at 707 East Franklin Street. Lyon Gardiner Tyler (2), who became president of William and Mary in 1888, founded the prestigious and scholarly *William and Mary Quarterly* as a private venture in 1892; it was absorbed by the college in 1919. Philip Alexander Bruce (3) wrote widely of colonial Virginia. Another well-known historian, Douglas Southall Freeman, wrote his Pulitzer Prize–winning biography, *R. E. Lee,* in his Richmond study (4).

4

1

2

Historic anniversaries and military reunions were always popular among descendants of Jamestown's pioneers. At Yorktown in 1931 (1), President Hoover was the speaker on the 150th anniversary of Cornwallis's surrender in 1781. To his left stood Marshal Henri Pétain of France. Victims of the siege (2) were unearthed in the gardens of the Governor's Palace at Williamsburg when the grounds were explored during the Rockefeller restoration, beginning in 1926; the palace had served as a hospital for French and American soldiers, many of whom died of smallpox. One of the last Confederate reunions, at Richmond in 1932 (3), brought out a few feeble veterans of the men in gray who had followed Robert E. Lee to Appomattox. Also gathered at the 1932 reunion were former Confederate soldiers' body servants (4).

3

4

1

Restoration

The 1920s spurred Virginia's consciousness of its past. In 1926 the Reverend William A. R. Goodwin, rector of Bruton Parish Church, persuaded John D. Rockefeller, Jr., to restore Williamsburg. The two men appear at left (1), with Goodwin holding a hat. The first building purchased was the Ludwell-Paradise House (2), on Duke of Gloucester Street near a vulcanizing shop. Years later the buildings had been restored (3). Meanwhile, archaeologists at Jamestown (4) excavated the site of America's first permanent English settlement. One of the structures renewed by Rockefeller was the Wren Building (5) of the College of William and Mary, which was restored to its 1718 appearance.

2

3

4

5

1

Many military bases encircled Chesapeake Bay to prepare men and material for service abroad in World War II. At a Virginia army base, trainees wore gas masks as they charged with bayonets under a smoke screen cover (1). At Newport News, the U.S.S. *Enterprise* (2), the first and most famous aircraft carrier to bear the name, was launched in 1936 with Mrs. Claude Swanson of Danville as sponsor; her husband was secretary of the navy. Army combat troops of the 45th Division were loaded aboard navy transports at Newport News on June 3, 1943 (3), to sail under convoy to the Mediterranean, where they invaded Sicily in the Allies' "Operation Husky," to free Europe of the Axis. Transports and cargo ships gathered in Hampton Roads (4) to sail under navy convoy and carry more American reinforcements to European and Pacific war zones.

2

Heroes and Visitors

4

5

Virginia's historic shrines have attracted many leaders over the years. In 1936, the Reverend W. A. R. Goodwin welcomed President and Mrs. Franklin Roosevelt (1) to Bruton Parish Church in Williamsburg. Ten years later, the Winston Churchills and the Dwight Eisenhowers (2), fresh from victory in World War II, visited the town. On the same tour, Churchill spoke to the General Assembly in Richmond, after being announced by the sergeant-at-arms of the House of Delegates (3). Queen Elizabeth, the Queen Mother (4), was welcomed to Jamestown in 1954 by Robert V. Hatcher and Delegate Lewis McMurran, chairmen of the federal and state bodies to plan the 350th year of Virginia's settlement. Queen Elizabeth II herself (5) spoke to a crowd of twenty-five thousand at Jamestown Festival Park in 1957 to mark England's advent in North America. In 1964, General Douglas MacArthur was interred (6) in Norfolk, where his mother had been born. The MacArthur Memorial was once Norfolk's City Hall, at the center of Virginia's largest metropolitan area.

313

6

The Changing Land

Long divided by rivers and mountain ranges, twentieth-century Virginia was newly united by a network of highways, bridges, and tunnels. Anticipating the interstate highway system, Virginia in 1954 opened the Shirley Highway (1) from the District of Columbia through Fairfax County. In the same period, Yorktown was linked to Gloucester with a bridge (2) over the York. In 1957, Norfolk and Hampton were joined by a bridge-tunnel across Hampton Roads. Sections of steel tubing for the tunnel were floated into place (3) and then submerged. The interior of a prefabricated section of tunnel was photographed in 1956 (4) as the work neared completion. In 1964, Virginia completed one of the world's most ambitious engineering feats: the 17.6-mile Chesapeake Bay Bridge-Tunnel, linking the Eastern Shore with Norfolk. This view (5) from Kiptopeke, the northern terminus, shows two of the bridge lifts as well as the connecting roadway leading to the long tunnel beneath Chesapeake Bay.

1

2

3

Eastern Virginia is part of a twentieth-century urban "corridor" along the coast from Boston to Norfolk. The once-dominant State Capitol is overwhelmed today by other buildings (1); the Jeffersonian masterpiece is visible at center of photograph, with Richmond's Coliseum in the mid-background. Around Hampton Roads (2), a cluster of streets links the growing cities of Norfolk, Portsmouth, Newport News, and Hampton. Hampton, the oldest continuously inhabited town in British North America, boasts a handsome new Coliseum (3), adjoining Virginia's busiest interstate highway and Hampton Roads Bridge-Tunnel. Farther north in the Atlantic coastal corridor stands Reston (4), the nation's first "planned community." Built near the District of Columbia, it combines fresh, modern design with rustic beauty, as at its J-shaped Lake Anne Village Center (5), where Restonites shop.

4

5   317

1

2

318

Virginia's strategic coastal location and its access to the District of Columbia brought it an increasing number of federal installations. At the Pentagon (1), on Virginia's bank of the Potomac at Washington, a navy helicopter prepares to land. Dulles Airport (2) was opened in northern Virginia in 1962. Its imposing building and imaginative layout were the work of architect Eero Saarinen. At NASA's Wallops Island Launch Facility, on the Eastern Shore, a missile (3) is prepared for launching. The first seven astronauts (4) arrived in 1959 at the National Aeronautics and Space Administration, Langley Field in Hampton. Seated are Virgil "Gus" Grissom, Scott Carpenter, Donald Slayton, and Gordon Cooper. Standing are Alan Shepard, Walter Schirra, and John Glenn. One of the navy's largest aircraft carriers (5) is carefully maneuvered into the Elizabeth River for overhaul at the naval shipyard at Portsmouth.

5

Champions

1

Although antibetting laws adopted in the 1790s discouraged high-stakes races, Virginia breeds and races some of America's finest horses. At the Warrenton Gold Cup, a race judge (1) scans the field. In 1973, the Virginia-bred Secretariat won the Belmont Stakes in New York to become one of the few "triple crown" heroes of turfdom. New York's then governor, Nelson Rockefeller (2), gives the Belmont Cup to Mrs. Penny Chenery Tweedy, Secretariat's owner, as jockey Ron Turcotte and Virginia's Governor Linwood Holton look on. In Hanover County, May is the time for the Camptown Races, whose stewards (3) patrol the track before starting time. Youngsters line the fence (4) at Camptown, while thousands of other spectators watch from a nearby hill. Thoroughbred breeding farms are numerous in northern Virginia and the Valley.

2

3

Stars

Star struck youngsters from the Old Dominion occasionally achieved renown in Hollywood and in New York. Richmond's Bill "Bojangles" Robinson (1) co-starred with Shirley Temple in the hit movie "The Little Colonel." Joseph Cotten (2) of Petersburg became a stage and screen hero, and George C. Scott (3) of Wise County an actor and director. Pearl Bailey (4) of Newport News sang her way to world fame. Shirley MacLaine (5) of northern Virginia went from the chorus line to movie eminence. The famous jazz singer Ella Fitzgerald (6) was born in Newport News in 1918, within a month of Pearl Bailey. Warren Beatty (7), brother of Shirley MacLaine, also became a headliner. In the realm of sports, Arthur Ashe, Jr., (8) of Richmond and Gum Springs became a tennis star, while Sam Snead (9), born at Hot Springs and later pro at White Sulphur, became a top tournament golfer of the 1940s and '50s.

5

6

7

8

9 323

A Setting for the Arts

4

5

The performing arts bloomed in twentieth-century Virginia as cities expanded. At Abingdon, the Barter Theatre (1) was founded during the Depression; farm produce was bartered for tickets. In 1947, Governor William M. Tuck (2) gave Helen Hayes a ham and an acre of land from Barter while founder-director Robert Porterfield looked on. The Stuttgart Ballet (3) fills the stage of Filene Center at northern Virginia's Wolf Trap Farm Park for the Performing Arts, near Dulles Airport. In Norfolk, a blighted city core was replaced by Scope, an ambitious center which includes Chrysler Hall, where director Russell Stanger (4) conducts a Norfolk Symphony rehearsal. Virginia in the 1930s created the Virginia Museum (5) in Richmond as the first state arts center in the United States. At Newport News, Archer and Anna Hyatt Huntington built the Mariners' Museum (6), whose collection relating to the seas is unexcelled.

6

Postwar Education

Schools grew bigger and more numerous each decade. At left, a rural youth is seen walking to school through a pine planting (1). Typical of modern schools is Hollin Hills School (2) in suburban Fairfax County, near Mount Vernon. At Episcopal High School in Alexandria, students and masters relax in front of Hoxton House (3), school headquarters. At Virginia Polytechnic Institute, the regimental band (4) was an important feature until military training was reduced. Mary Baldwin College (5) at Staunton typifies the traditional Virginia women's school. Less traditional was a women's teacher-training college at Harrisonburg, which grew into the modern coeducational Madison College (6). The former residence of novelist Ellen Glasgow in Richmond (7) served, after her death, as the University Center of Virginia.

5

6

7

1

2

3

Controversy Over Integration

Linwood Holton of Big Stone Gap took oath as governor (1) in 1970—the first Republican in that office since 1886; Virginia's Chief Justice Harold Snead administered the oath as the outgoing Governor Mills E. Godwin, Jr., looked on. Four years later, Godwin succeeded Holton (2)—the first Virginia governor since the Civil War to be elected for two terms. During Holton's tenure, the governor walked his daughter (3) to Richmond's John F. Kennedy High School for its September opening, supporting the federally ordered busing plan; this picture, front-paged in the *New York Times,* recorded "the most significant happening in this Commonwealth during my lifetime," wrote ex-Governor Colgate Darden, Jr. The photograph above (4) shows school buses caught in traffic while taking children to an integrated school. Many people fought busing, as did these pickets in Newport News (5), but the integration of Virginia's schools continued (6).

4

5

6

Affairs of State

Politics—once a "gentleman's game"—became increasingly intense as Virginia became a two-party state in the 1970s. Chief executives of the Old Dominion gathered in Roanoke in 1970 (1). Standing are William Tuck of Halifax, Colgate Darden, Jr., of Norfolk, Albertis Harrison, Jr., of Brunswick, and J. Lindsay Almond, Jr., of Roanoke. Seated are Thomas B. Stanley of Henry, Mills E. Godwin, Jr., of Nansemond, and John S. Battle of Charlottesville—all postwar occupants of the Governor's Office (2). The Governor's Mansion (3) has been used by chief executives since Monroe's day. Virginia political affairs were observed for years by Fred Seibel (4), whose cartoons enlivened the *Richmond Times-Dispatch*. In 1949, Seibel showed anti-organization Democrat Francis Pickens Miller (5) attempting to storm the Bastille of the Byrd organization. In the 1950s, he frequently dealt with the race issue, as in this drawing (6) of sectional differences over school integration.

2

3

Industry Today

7

Rural interests dominated Virginia until World War II, but industry now reigns. Especially in the eastern urban corridor, factories and population have grown. Along the James in lower Richmond, this row of tobacco manufactories (1) fills the air with pungent odors. Danville (2) is one of the nation's textile centers and home of Dan River Mills. In Chesterfield County sprawls the huge plant of E. I. duPont de Nemours (3). Mining (4) is an important industry in southwest Virginia, where rich beds of fossil fuel abound in Appalachia. In Tazewell County, the Jewell Ridge Coal Mine (5) produces fuel to be hauled by rail to Hampton Roads ports. At Newport News (6), coal piers and ship repair docks project like fingers into the James River; the yard can now handle nuclear-fueled vessels. The largest passenger ship ever built by an American yard is the S.S. *United States* (7), being escorted from her builders' yards at Newport News in 1952.

1

Agricultural Riches

Mechanization slowly changed tobacco growing, but leaves continued to be cured on lathes in barns (1). Throughout the Southside tobacco belt, bidders vie for the best leaves (2). In the uplands around Winchester, apples grow abundantly (3), and in the Tidewater flatlands, truck crops like butterbeans (4) are harvested. Watermen catch hard crabs (5) and keep them in floats to "bust" into soft crabs. The netting of menhaden (6) has become a major Chesapeake industry.

2

3

4

5

6

2

One Virginia region where life has changed little over the years is the Eastern Shore. The famous annual roundup of wild ponies at Assateague (1) has been a tradition for many decades. Tangier Island (2), settled by fishermen in the seventeenth century and still a fishing community, remains almost as it was in the nineteenth century.

The Past and the Present

The more Virginia changes, the more it stays the same. The visible links between 1607 and the 1970s are abundant. The heart of Virginia's tradition is its Capitol, at Richmond, where stands Houdon's sculpture of George Washington (1), copied from life. In Williamsburg, wigs are still made (2) and fitted to the wearer. In Gloucester County, the modest birthplace of Walter Reed (3), conqueror of yellow fever, is maintained for visitors. At Carter's Grove near Williamsburg, Mr. and Mrs. Archibald McCrea (4) are shown proudly exhibiting their restoration of the house. A grim reminder of World War I is the Tomb of the Unknown Soldier (5), which speaks a nation's gratitude to the military men buried in Arlington National Cemetery. In the yard of Bruton Parish Church in Williamsburg (6), visitors read the faded script of an eighteenth-century tombstone. All contribute to the pride, the legend, that make Virginia an unchanging spirit in modern America.

Bibliography

Print and Photographic Archives

The following collections were used in an effort to obtain the most complete record available of Virginia's past and present: Association for the Preservation of Virginia Antiquities, Richmond; Colonial Williamsburg Foundation, Williamsburg; Daily Press Incorporated, Newport News; Jamestown Foundation, Jamestown; Library of Congress, Washington, D.C.; Mariners Museum, Newport News; Southwest Virginia Museum, Big Stone Gap; Valentine Museum, Richmond, including photographic prints and negatives extending from the Civil War to the early twentieth century in Virginia, made by George Cook, his son, Huestis Cook, and others; Virginia Historical Society, Richmond, including the Michael Miley photographic collection of nineteenth-century Lexington and the Foster Studio collection, chiefly of Richmond subjects, extending from the late nineteenth-century photographs of Walter Washington Foster to the twentieth-century photographs of his son-in-law and successor, Arthur Orpin; Virginia State Chamber of Commerce, Richmond, consisting of photographs of industry, agriculture, maritime life, and public affairs since 1924, most of them by Philip Flournoy; and Virginia State Library, Richmond, whose graphic files touch nearly every phase of Virginia life.

Books and Magazines

American Heritage, Editors. *The American Heritage History of American Antiques.* New York: American Heritage Publishing Co., 1968.

————. *The American Heritage History of the American People.* New York: American Heritage Publishing Co., 1970.

————. *The American Heritage History of the Thirteen Colonies.* New York: American Heritage Publishing Co., 1967.

American Tobacco Company. *"Sold American!": The First Fifty Years.* New York: American Tobacco Company, 1954.

BEYER, EDWARD. *Album of Virginia.* Richmond: Virginia Enquirer Printing Office, 1858.

BODINE, AUBREY. *The Face of Virginia.* 1967.

BROWN, ALEXANDER CROSBY, ed. *Newport News' 326 Years.* Newport News: The Golden Anniversary Corporation, 1946.

BUCHANAN, LAMONT. *A Pictorial History of the Confederacy.* New York: Crown Publishers, 1951.

BUTTERFIELD, ROGER. *The American Past.* New York: Simon and Schuster, 1947.

DABNEY, VIRGINIUS. *Virginia, the New Dominion.* Garden City: Doubleday, 1971.

FISHWICK, MARSHALL. *General Lee's Photographer.* Chapel Hill: University of North Carolina Press, 1954.

GUERNSEY, ALFRED H., and ALDEN, HENRY M. *Harper's Pictorial History of the Great Rebellion,* 2 vols. New York: Harper and Brothers, 1868.

HORAN, JAMES D. *Mathew Brady, Historian with a Camera.* New York: Bonanza Books, 1955.

HOWE, HENRY. *Historical Collections of Virginia.* Charleston: Babcock and Company, 1854.

KANE, HARNETT. *Gone Are the Days: An Illustrated History of the Old South.* New York: Dutton, 1960.

KOCHER, LAWRENCE, and DEARSTYNE, HOWARD. *Shadows in Silver: A Record of Virginia, 1850–1900.* New York: Scribners, 1954.

KOUWENHOVEN, JOHN A. *Adventures of America, 1857–1900: A Pictorial Record from Harper's Weekly.* New York: Harper and Brothers, 1938.

LEYBURN, JAMES G. *The Scotch-Irish: A Social History.* Chapel Hill: University of North Carolina Press, 1962.

MIDDLETON, ARTHUR PIERCE. *Tobacco Coast.* Newport News: The Mariners Museum, 1953.

MORTON, RICHARD LEE. *Colonial Virginia,* 2 vols. Chapel Hill: University of North Carolina Press, 1960.

NEWHALL, BEAUMONT. *The Daguerreotype in America.* New York: Duell, Sloan & Pearce, 1961.

O'NEAL, WILLIAM B. *Pictorial History of the University of Virginia.* Charlottesville: University Press of Virginia, 1968.

PRATT, FLETCHER. *Civil War in Pictures.* New York: Henry Holt and Co., 1955.

QUENNELL, MARJORIE, and QUENNELL, C. H. B. *A History of Everyday Things in England,* vol. 2. New York: G. P. Putnam's Sons, 1965.

RENIERS, PERCEVAL. *The Springs of Virginia.* Chapel Hill: University of North Carolina Press, 1941.

ROUSE, PARKE, JR. *Below the James Lies Dixie.* Richmond: Dietz Press, 1968.

———. *Cows on the Campus.* Richmond: Dietz Press, 1973.

———. *Endless Harbor: The Story of Newport News.* Newport News: Newport News Historical Committee, 1969.

———. *The Great Wagon Road.* New York: McGraw-Hill, 1973.

———. *Planters and Pioneers: Life in Colonial Virginia.* New York: Hastings House, 1968.

———. *Virginia: The English Heritage in America.* New York: Hastings House, 1966.

SIMKINS, FRANCIS BUTLER, and HUNNICUTT, SPOTSWOOD. *Virginia: History, Government, Geography.* New York: Scribners, 1957.

Valentine Museum. *Fifty Years in Richmond, 1898–1948.* Richmond: Whittet and Shepperson, 1948.

Virginia Cavalcade (quarterly). Volume 1 (Summer 1951) to date. Richmond: Virginia State Library.

WEDDELL, ALEXANDER WILBOURNE. *Richmond Virginia in Old Prints, 1737–1887.* Richmond. Johnson Publishing Company, 1932.

———. *Virginia Historical Portraiture, 1585–1930.* Richmond: William Byrd Press, 1930.

WERTENBAKER, THOMAS JEFFERSON. *Norfolk: Historic Southern Port.* Durham: Duke University Press, 1962.

342

Picture Credits

Here is a list of abbreviations used in the picture credits:

APVA: Association for the Preservation of Virginia Antiquities
BM: British Museum, London
CSS: Charles Scribner's Sons art files
CW: Colonial Williamsburg
HW: *Harper's Weekly*
ILN: *Illustrated London News*
LC: Library of Congress
Leslie's: *Frank Leslie's Illustrated Newspaper*
NA: National Archives
NPS: National Park Service
NYPL: New York Public Library
SM: *Scribner's Monthly*
VDCD: Virginia Department of Conservation and Development
VHS: Virginia Historical Society, Richmond
VM: Valentine Museum, Richmond
VSCC: Virginia State Chamber of Commerce
VSL: Virginia State Library, Richmond
VSTS: Virginia State Travel Service

20–21 1. Photo: M. E. Warren. 2. Photo: Post-Wolcott, October 1940. LC. 3. VSTS. 4. Norfolk and Western Railway. 22–23 Photo: Post-Wolcott, May 1941. LC. 24–25 1,4. VSTS. 2. CSS. 3. VSCC. 26–27 1–3. John Smith, *Generall Historie*, 1624. 4,5. Engraving by G. Veen. DeBry *Virginia*. BM. 6. Ashmolean Museum, Oxford. 7. Copperplate engraving by W. Hollar, 1645. BM. 28–29 1. VSL. 2. Attributed to M. Gheeraedts. National Portrait Gallery, London. 3. Artist unknown. National Portrait Gallery, London. 4. NYPL, Rare Book Division. 30–31 1,2. John Smith, *Generall Historie*, 1624. 3. VSL. 4. Engraving by Simon Vande Passe. CW. 5. By courtesy of The Society of Antiquaries of London. 6. Edward Williams, *Virgo Triumphans: or Virginia Richly and Truly Valued*, London, 1650. 32–33 1,2. John Smith, *Generall Historie*, 1632. 3. Robert Vaughan, "Graven and extracted out of generall historie of Virginia, New England, and some Isles." 34–35 1–5. NPS. Colonial National Historic Park, Yorktown. 36–37 1. Artist unknown. Copy of original painting owned by Sir Edmund Lechmare. Courtesy, The Jamestown Foundation. 2. Public Record Office: C.O. 1/1 No. 45. 3. Artist unknown. The Virginia Museum of Fine Arts, Richmond. 4,6,7. VHS. 5. CSS. 38–39 1,3,5. Photo: Phil Flournoy. VSCC. 2. LC. 4. APVA. 40–41 1. VSL. 2–5. Ingham Foster Collection, Imperial Tobacco Com-

pany, Bristol, England. 42–43 1. Gottfried, *Historie Antipodum . . . Newe Welt*, 1631. 2. Stow, *Survey of London*, 1633. VSL. 3. VSL. 4. VHS. 5. Photo: Thomas L. Williams. Courtesy, College of William and Mary, Williamsburg. 6. Portrait by Hargreaves. Courtesy, College of William and Mary, Williamsburg. 44–45 1. From Rutherfoord Goodwin, *Williamsburg in Virginia*, 1710. CW. 2,3. Sketch by Franz Ludwig Michel, 1702. CW. 4. CW. 5. VM. 6. From original miniature by J. Smart. Now in possession of Gerald E. Fauquier, Rockcliffe, Ottawa, Canada. 7. VHS. 46–47 1–3. Photo: Thomas L. Williams. CW. 4. Photo: Charles Larson. CW. 5. CW. 48–49 1,2. Photo: Thomas L. Williams. CW. 50–51 1. VSCC. 2. Photo: Thomas L. Williams. CW. 3,4. CW. 5. Painting by Charles W. Peale. CW. 6. *Virginia Gazette*, August 28, 1752. 52–53 1. Photo: Phil Flournoy. VSCC. 2. VSCC. 3,4. VDCD. 5. CSS. 6. Painting by George Stubbs, 1775. National Gallery of Art, Collection of Mr. and Mrs. Paul Mellon. 54–55 Artist unknown, American, ca. 1780. National Gallery of Art, Garbisch Collection. 56–57 1. Map by Joshua Fry and Peter Jefferson, 1751. Duke University Library, Durham, N.C. 2. Ingham Foster Collection, Imperial Tobacco Company, Bristol, England. 3. LC. 4. NPS. 5. NYPL, Reserve Division. 6. Courtesy, College of William and Mary Library, Williamsburg. 7. CSS. 58–59 1. Collection of Mrs. James H. Oliver. Courtesy, Frick Art Reference Library. 2,3. VSL. 4. Portrait by Sir Godfrey Kneller. VM. 5. Engraving by Byrd, ca. 1738. Bodleian Library, Oxford. 6. VDCD. 7. VSTS. 60–61 1. Courtesy, Fontaine Maury Watson estate. 2. Courtesy, Mrs. Rebecca Ingles Steele. 3. VSL. 4. Courtesy, Waterford Foundation, Inc. 5–7. LC. 62–63 1. Engraved by Thomas Jeffreys after a map by John Henry. CW. 2. Engraved by Lewis after a painting by Chester Harding. Missouri Historical Society. 3. VSCC. 4. Photo: Phil Flournoy. VSCC. 64–65 1. Photo: Thomas C. Bradshaw II, Lexington. 2. Courtesy, Lexington Presbyterian Church and Washington and Lee University, Lexington. 3. *Virginia Gazette*, September 1775. VSL. 4. Hampden-Sydney College. 5. APVA. 6. VSL. 66–67 1. Portrait by Charles W. Peale, 1772. Courtesy, Washington and Lee University, Lexington. 2. VDCD. 3,5. LC. 4. VM. 6. George Washington, 1754. BM. 68–69 1. Artist unknown, American, ca. 1725. Courtesy, Washington and Lee University, Lexington, The Washington-Curtis-Lee Collection. 2. Artist unknown, American, ca. 1722. The Virginia Museum of Fine Arts. 3. Artist unknown. National Gallery of Art, Garbisch Collection. 4. Watercolor by G. Tobin. National Maritime Museum, Greenwich, England. Photo: Courtesy, The Mariner's Museum, Newport News. 5. *Pennsylvania Gazette*,

October 27, 1748. 70–71 1,3. CW. 2. Collection of Charles W. and Julia Wickham Porter. VM. 4. VSL. 5. NYPL, Picture Collection. 6. *Virginia Gazette,* November 30, 1759. 7. Courtesy, The Homestead, Hot Springs. 72–73 1,4,5. CW. 2,3. Photo: Phil Flournoy. VSCC. 74–75 1. Courtesy, Mrs. Charles Murray. Reproduced by permission of the Scottish National Portrait Gallery, Edinburgh. 2,3,5. CW. 4. Original in State Capitol, Richmond. 6,7. VSL. 8. VDCD. 76–77 1. Painting by John Trumbull. Yale University Art Gallery. 2. LC. 3. Miniature by Charles W. Peale, 1777. Metropolitan Museum of Art, Gift of William H. Huntington. 78–79 1. VSL. 2. VM. 3. Stipple engraving by D. Edwin after Barralet. Published by James Webster, 1814. LC. 4. Painting by Alonzo Chappel. VSL. 5. NA. 6. CW. 80–81 1. Portrait by James Northcote. National Maritime Museum, Greenwich. 2. Painting by Théodore Gudin. Musée de Versailles. 3. National Maritime Museum, Greenwich. 4. CW. 82–83 1. CW. 2. Detail of gouache by Henri-Désiré van Blarenberghe, 1784. Musée de Versailles. 3. VHS. 4. Watercolor by Benjamin Latrobe. VSL. 5. NPS. 84–85 Painting by John Trumbull. Office of the Architect of the Capitol. LC. 86–87 1. Courtesy, Collection of W. Palmer Grey. 2. Print by Cailleau, Paris, 1788. Virginia Museum of Fine Arts. 3. Drawing by Peter Maverick, *The Letters of a British Spy.* VM. 4. VSL. 5. Photo: Phil Flournoy. VSCC. 88–89 1. Portrait by Gilbert Stuart. White House Collection. Courtesy, Frick Art Reference Library. 2,4. The Mount Vernon Ladies' Association. 3. Drawing by George Washington, 1793. Henry E. Huntington Library and Art Gallery. 5. Photo: Samuel Chamberlain. The Mount Vernon Ladies' Association. 6. Painting by Benjamin Latrobe. Collection of James W. Tucker, Alexandria. 7. Sculpture by T. Clarke, Boston, 1801. NYPL, Print Collection. 90–91 1. Portrait by Charles W. Peale. Independence National Historic Park Collection. 2. Artist unknown, ca. 1826. Collection of T. Jefferson Coolidge, Jr. 3. Thomas Jefferson Memorial Foundation, Monticello. 4. Plan by Thomas Jefferson. Thomas Jefferson Memorial Foundation, Monticello. 5. News Service. University of Virginia. 92–93 1. Papers of George Washington. LC. 2. LC. 3. Portrait by J. W. Jarvis. Collection of Richard Coke Marshall. Courtesy, Frick Art Reference Library. 94–95 1,2. Photo: Marler. VSTS. 3–5. VSTS. 96–97 1,2. From William Tatham, *An Historical and Pictorial Essay,* London, 1800. NYPL, Rare Book Division. 3. Courtesy, The New York Historical Society. 98–99 1. Portrait by Gilbert Stuart. Bowdoin College Museum of Fine Arts. 2. Portrait by Rembrandt Peale. Courtesy, The New York Historical Society. 3. VSL. 4. Engraving by William Charles. LC. 5. Courtesy, The New York Historical Society. 100–101 1. Photo: Thomas L. Williams. CW. 2. Wm. and Mary. 3. Watercolor by James Seymour. Collection of the late Willard S. Martin. 4,5. VSL. 102–103 Copper engraving by Andrew Henkel, 1810. Collection of Klaus Wust. 2. Collection of Klaus Wust. 3. Courtesy, Roderick Moore, Ferrum. 4. Peter Bernhart. Courtesy, Menno Simons Library, Eastern Mennonite College, Harrisonburg. 5. Abby Aldrich Rockefeller Folk Art Collection. 104–105 1. Portrait by Thomas Sully. West Point Museum Collections. U.S. Military Academy. 2,4,5. VSL. 3. University of Virginia Library. 106–107 Painting by George Catlin. VSL. 108–109 1. NYPL, Stokes Collection. 2–4. VSL. 110–111 1,2. VSL. 3. Alderman Library, U. of Virginia. 4. Painting by Bethual Moore. Photo: Thomas L. Williams. Courtesy, College of William and Mary, Williamsburg. 5. News Bureau. College of William and Mary, Williamsburg. 6. Photo: Thomas L. Williams. 112–113 1. VSL.

2–4. Engraving by A. B. Walter. VSL. 5. Pencil drawing by Charles P. Deyerle, ca. 1841. Virginia Military Institute Museum. 6. Randolph-Macon College. 7. Original from Henry Howe, *Historical Collections of Virginia,* 1849. Courtesy, Washington and Lee University, Lexington. 114–115 1. Courtesy, College of William and Mary, Williamsburg. 2. Artist unknown, ca. 1810. Collection of Edgar W. and Bernice C. Garbisch. 116–117 1. Sketch by Benjamin Latrobe, *The Papers of Benjamin Henry Latrobe.* Courtesy, The Maryland Historical Society, Baltimore. 2. Samuel Warner, *Authentic and Impartial Narrative of the Tragical Scene,* 1831. LC. 3,4. *Lewis Miller Sketch Book,* ca. 1853. Collection of George Hay Kain. VSL. 118–119 1. Painting by Junius Brutus Stearns, 1851. Virginia Museum of Fine Arts, Gift of Colonel and Mrs. Edgar W. Garbisch. 2. LC. 3,4. CSS. 120–121 1. Engraving from Morrison, *Guide to the City of Washington,* 1844. LC. 2–5. VSL. 122–123 Henry Howe, *Historical Collections of Virginia,* 1849. VSL. 124–125 1. *Naval Chronicle,* London, 1815. Courtesy, The Mariner's Museum, Newport News. 2. Lithograph by G. Lehman from a sketch by Joseph G. Braff. Courtesy, Portsmouth Naval Shipyard Museum. 3. VSL. 4. Henry Howe, *Historical Collections of Virginia,* 1849. CSS. 5. Henry Howe, *Historical Collections of Virginia,* 1849. VSL. 6. Bronze casting of original carving by William Luke. Courtesy, U.S. Naval Academy, Annapolis. 126–127 1. Edward Beyer, *Album of Virginia.* 2. VSTS. 3. VSL. 128–129 1. Edward Beyer, *Album of Virginia.* VSL. 2,3,5. VSL. 4. Courtesy, The Mariner's Museum, Newport News. 130–131 1. CSS. 2. VSL. 3. NA. 4. Courtesy, Washington and Lee University, Lexington. 5. International Harvester Co., Chicago. 6. Photo: Phil Flournoy. VSCC. 132–133 1. NYPL, I. N. Phelps Stokes Collection. 2,4. VSL. 3. Edward Beyer, *Album of Virginia.* VSL. 5. ILN, March 9, 1861. 134–135 1. Courtesy, U.S. Bureau of Engraving and Printing. 2,3. VM. 4. VDCD. 5. LC. 6,7. VSL. 136–137 1–3. HW, June 27, 1857. VSL. 138–139 1,5. VM. 2–4. VSL. 6. VDCD. 140–141 1,4. VSL. 2,7. LC. 3. Sketch by Porte Crayon. HW, November 5, 1859. 5. Sketch by Porte Crayon. HW, November 12, 1859. Courtesy, The New York Historical Society. 6. *Leslie's,* December 17, 1859. 142–143 1,2. CSS. 3. NA. 4. U.S. War Department General Staff. Photo No. 165-C-518, NA. 5. VSL. 144–145 HW, June 8, 1861. VSL. 146–147 1. Drawing by Eyre Crowe, 1853. VM. 2. Photo: Mathew Brady, ca. 1859. NA. 3. Richmond Chamber of Commerce. 4. HW, May 31, 1862. Courtesy, The New York Historical Society. 5. ILN, July 27, 1861. 148–149 1. Benson J. Lossing, *Pictorial Field Book of the Civil War,* vol. 1, 1868. 2. Courtesy, Portsmouth Naval Shipyard Museum. 3. *Leslie's,* April 30, 1861. 150–151 1. CSS. 2. Watercolor by G. Kaiser, 1862. Courtesy, The Mariner's Museum, Newport News. 3,4. VSL. 5. *Leslie's,* June 22, 1861. 152–153 1. *Leslie's,* August 3, 1861. 2. ILN, November 23, 1861. 3. Photo: Herb Peck, Jr., Nashville. 4. HW. 5. LC. 154–155 1. *Harper's History of the Great Rebellion,* May, 1862. 2. *New York Illustrated News,* September 30, 1861. 3. LC. 4. Photo: Mathew Brady. LC. 156–157 Lithograph by Henry Bill, 1862. Courtesy, The Mariner's Museum, Newport News. 158–159 1. U.S. Signal Corp. Photo No. 111-B-5867, Brady Collection, NA. 2. *Leslie's,* 1862. 3. Photo: Mathew Brady. LC. 4. Engraving by H. B. Halts Sons, N.Y. 5. Courtesy, Museum of Fine Arts, Boston. 6. Sketch by J. Mertz, 1862. LC. 160–161 1. Self-portrait by Conrad Wise Chapman. VM. 2. HW, August 16, 1862. 3. HW, July 19, 1862. Courtesy, The New York Historical Society. 4. CSS. 5. *Leslie's,* August 2, 1862. 162–163

1–4. VSL.   5. *Leslie's,* June 15, 1861.   **164–165**
1. Photo: Michael Moley. VHS. 2. Painting by David
Gilmeur Blyth. Courtesy, Museum of Fine Arts, Boston,
M. and M. Karolik Collection. 3. Sketch by W. C.
Schwartzburg, ca. 1864. LC. 4. HW, September 20, 1862.
5. CSS.   **166–167** 1. LC. 2,3. Courtesy, Confederate
Museum, Richmond. 4. HW, April 12, 1862. 5. *Leslie's,*
July 5, 1862. 6. HW, May 23, 1863.   **168–169** 1. HW,
June 14, 1862. 2. LC. 3. NYPL, Rare Book Division. 4.
Photo: J. and A. Gardner, 1864.   **170–171** 1,4–6. CSS.
2. *Leslie's,* 1862. 3. NA.   **172–173** 1. HW, 1861. 2.
VSL. 3. Print of original portrait owned by Dr. Neil P.
Campbell. 4. Alderman Library, U. of Virginia. 5.
HW, October 10, 1863.   **174–175** 1,3,5. VSL. 2.
VM. 4. Photo: Mathew Brady. VSL. 6,7. Photo:
George S. Cook. CSS.   **176–177** 1. Pen drawing by
William L. Sheppard. VM. 2. Benson J. Lossing, *Pictorial
Field Book of the Civil War,* vol. II, 1868. 3. CSS. 4,6.
VSL. 5. Chase Manhattan Bank Museum of Moneys of the
World.   **178–179** 1. HW. 2. *Harper's Pictorial History
of the Great Rebellion,* 1866. VSL. 3. Pratt, *Civil War in
Pictures,* 1864. 4. New Market Battlefield Park. 5. HW,
September 5, 1863.   **180–181** 1. *Leslie's,* October 29,
1864. 2. *Leslie's,* November 12, 1864.   **182–183** 1–4.
VSL. 5. LC.   **184–185** 1. CSS. 2–6. VSL.   **186–187**
1–3. VSL. 4. ILN, October 22, 1864. 5. LC.   **188–189**
1. VHS. 2,6 LC. 3. Engraving by A. H. Ritchie. VSL. 4.
Sketch by A. R. Waud. Pierpont Morgan Collection. LC.
5. CSS. 7. HW, 1865.   **190–191** 1. Photo: Mathew
Brady. 2,4,5. LC. 3. Photo: Mathew Brady. NA.
192–193 1–4. VSL. 5. CSS.   **194–195** Sketch by Joseph
Becker.   **196–197** 1. Lithograph by Kimmel and Forster,
1865. LC. 2. U.S. Signal Corp. Photo No. 111-B-4055,
Brady Collection, NA. 3. LC. 4,5. CSS. 6. HW, 1866. VSL.
198–199 1,2. VSL. 3. HW, November 4, 1865. 4.
Courtesy, Washington and Lee University, Lexington. 5.
Photo: Mathew Brady, LC.   **200–201** 1. Drawing by
J. R. Chapin. LC. 2. Drawing by A. R. Waud. LC. 3.
LC.   **202–203** 1. ILN, July 22, 1865. 2. HW, October
14, 1865. 3,5. VSL. 4. Fort Monroe Casemate Museum.
6. Pencil sketch by A. R. Waud. Pierpont-Morgan Collection. LC. 7. *Leslie's.* VSL.   **204–205** 1,2. Photo: Wiley.
3,4. Courtesy, Greenbrier Hotel, White Sulphur Springs.
5. CSS. 6. Courtesy, Washington and Lee University, Lexington. 7. VSL.   **206–207** 1,6,7. VM. 2–4. HW. VSL.
5. Sketch by Dr. Bracket, July 11, 1867. Courtesy, Confederate Museum, Richmond.   **208–209** 1,2. VSL. 3.
HW, 1870. VSL.   **210–211** 1. HW, October 14, 1865.
VM. 2–4. VSL. 5. CSS.   **212–213** HW, November 7,
1868.   **214–215** 1. VM. 2–4. VSL. 5. Norfolk and
Western Railway. 6. VHS. 7. *Leslie's,* June 25, 1881.
VSL.   **216–217** 1. SM, April 1874. 2. HW, December
31, 1870. VM. 3. CSS. 4. Courtesy, Mrs. V. Lee Kirby,
Williamsburg. 5. Photo: James Mooney, 1900. Smithsonian
Institution, National Anthropological Archives, Bureau of
American Ethnology Collection. 6. NPS.   **218–219** 1.
HW, 1870. VSL. 2. Painting by Richard N. Brooke, 1881.
Corcoran Gallery of Art.   **220–221** 1. Photo: Huestis
P. Cook. VM. 2. *Leslie's.* VSL.   **222–223** 1,2. VSL.
3–5,7. LC. 6. Office of Public Relations, Hampton Institute,
Hampton.   **224–225** 1–8. SM, April 1874.   **226–
227** 1. Henry Linton, *Picturesque America.* NYPL. 2.
Henry Linton, *Picturesque America,* 1872–1874. NYPL.
3. HW, 1873. VSL. 4. VSL.   **228–229** 1. *New York
Daily Graphic,* October 22, 1881. 2,4. VSL. 3. NA. 5.
CSS.   **230–231** 1. Virginia Polytechnic Institute. 2,7.
CW. 3. Virginia Military Institute. 4,5. VSL. 6. Hampton
Institute, Hampton.   **232–233** 1–5. CW.   **234–235**
1–3. VSL. 4. *Leslie's,* October 19, 1889. VSL. 5. LC. 6.

C & O *Railway Directory,* 1881–1882. VSL.   **236–237**
1. VM. 2,4,5. VSL. 3. Norfolk and Western Railway.
238–239 1–5. VM.   **240–241** 1. VM. 2. HW, December
4, 1886. 3. HW, vii, p. 253, 1867. 4. VSL. 5. *The Daily
Crimson,* Friday, October 4, 1889.   **242–243** 1. HW,
January 15, 1887. LC. 2. SM, April 1874. 3. VM.
244–245 1,5. CSS. 2. VM. 3. Photo: Huestis P. Cook. VM.
4. Edward Pollock, *Historical and Industrial Guide to
Petersburg,* Virginia, 1884. VSL.   **246–247** VSL.
248–249 Drawn by Major William H. Blow. Courtesy,
The Swem Library, College of William and Mary, Williamsburg.   **250–251** 1,5. CW. 2. Courtesy, The Mariner's Museum, Newport News. 3,4. VM.   **252–253**
Photo: George S. Cook. CSS.   **254–255** 1. VHS. 2.
Painting by A. Fisher, VHS. 3. Photo: George S. Cook. CSS.
4,5. VM.   **256–257** 1. Courtesy, Ellen M. Bogly. 2. VSL.
3–5. VHS. 6. Photo: Gertrude Kasebier. 7. Private Collec-
tion.   **258–259** 1. CW. 2. VM. 3. VSL. 4. Hampton
Institute, Hampton. 5. VHS.   **260–261** 1,3. CW. 2.
Photo: courtesy, Mrs. V. Lee Kirby, Williamsburg. 4.
Courtesy, College of William and Mary, Williamsburg.
5. Photo: courtesy, Mary Mordecai Goodwin. 6. Courtesy,
Jamestown Foundation. 7. VM.   **262–263** 1,2. VM. 3.
Photo: Michael Miller. VHS. 4. CSS.   **264–265** 1. VSL.
2. VM. 3,5. Courtesy, The Mariner's Museum, Newport
News. 4. Courtesy, Newport News Shipbuilding and Dry
Dock Co. Copied by The Mariner's Museum, Newport
News.   **266–267** 1,3. VSL. 2. Courtesy, The Mariner's
Museum, Newport News.   **268–269** 1–3. LC.   **270–
271** 1. Olinedinst Studio. 2. Oil painting by Thomas C.
Skinner. Courtesy, The Mariner's Museum, Newport News.
3. Photo: Rusk and Shaw, 1898. Courtesy, The Mariner's
Museum, Newport News. 4. Photo: George F. Shaver.
VM.   **272–273** 1. A. T. & T. 2,5. NYPL, Picture Col-
lection. 3. VM. 4. Photo: Huestis P. Cook. VM. 6. Photo:
Jim Corbett. VSCC.   **274–275** 1. VHS. 2,4,5. VM. 3.
Walter Reed AMC Communications Photo Facility. 6.
VSL.   **276–277** 1–4,6. VM. 5. VSL.   **278–279**
VSL.   **280–281** 1. Collection of Carroll Walker, Nor-
folk. 2. Collection of Louisa Venable Kyle, Virginia Beach.
3. VHS. 4. Courtesy, The Mariner's Museum. Newport
News. **282–283** 1. LC. 2,3. VHS. **284–285** 1,4,5. Virginia
Dept. of Highways. 2. Collection of Fred Painter. 3.
Photo: Caldwell. Virginia Dept. of Highways.   **286–
287** 1. George C. Marshall Research Library. 2. Courtesy,
The George C. Marshall Research Foundation. 3. University of Virginia, Dept. of Graphics. 4. Courtesy, Woodrow
Wilson Foundation, Staunton. 5. Smithsonian Institution.
288–289 1. VSL. 2. U.S. Signal Corp. Photo. No.
111-SC-56953, NA. 3. Courtesy, Newport News Shipbuilding and Dry Dock Co. 4. LC. 5. The American Red Cross.
6. U.S. Signal Corp. Photo. No. 111-RB-826, NA.
290–291 1,2. National Tobacco-Textile Museum, Danville.
3. Syms-Eaton Museum, Hampton. 4. Collection of John
Mitchell.   **292–293** 1,2. VHS. 3,4. National Tobacco-
Textile Museum, Danville. 5. Virginia Dept. of Highways.
294–295 1. Courtesy, Dr. Janet Kimbrough, Williamsburg. 2. Photo: Phil Flournoy. VSCC. 3. VDCD. 4.
CSS. 5. University of Virginia. 6. Courtesy, Washington
and Lee University, Lexington. 7 University of Richmond.
296–297 1,2. VSL. 3. Southwest Virginia Museum,
Big Stone Gap. 4. CSS. 5. Randolph-Macon Woman's
College, Lynchburg. 6. Photo: Dave Greear. Sherwood
Anderson Papers. The Newberry Library, Chicago. 7. VHS.
8. VM.   **298–299** 1. Smithsonian Institution, National
Anthropological Archives. 2,3. Collection of Powell Glass,
Lynchburg. 4. Photo: Crosscup & West End Co., Phila-
delphia. VSL. 5. VSL. 6,7. Dementi Studio, Richmond.
300–301 1. VHS. 2. Photo: A. Rothstein. LC. 3. VSL.

4. CSS. 5. Official Corp. of Engineers Photo. Courtesy, The District Engineer, U.S. Engineer District, Wilmington, N.C.   302–303 1,2. Southwest Virginia Museum, Big Stonè Gap. 3. Collection of Phyllis Stephenson. 4,5. NPS. Courtesy, Superintendent, Shenandoah National Park, Luray.   304–305 1,3. VHS. 2. Courtesy, College of William and Mary, Williamsburg. 4. Dementi Studio, Richmond.   306–307 1. Dementi Studio, Richmond. 2. CW. 3,4. VHS.   308–309 1,2. CW. 3,5. Photo: Thomas L. Williams. CW. 4. VSL.   310–311 1. U.S. Army Photo. 2. Courtesy, Newport News Shipbuilding and Dry Dock Co. 3. Courtesy, The Mariner's Museum, Newport News. 4. U.S. Navy Dept. Photo. No. 80-G-355116, NA. 312–313 1,2. CW.   3. Courtesy, Miss Delia E. Brock, Hampden-Sydney. 4,5. Courtesy, Jamestown Foundation. 6. *Norfolk Virginian.*   314–315 1. Photo: Jesse L. Ailstock. Virginia Dept. of Highways. 2. Photo: Phil Flournoy. VSCC. 3–5. Chesapeake Bay Bridge-Tunnel, Cape Charles.   316–317 1. Al Cothran Studio. 2. Photo: Phil Flournoy. VSCC. 3. Photo: Gordon H. Schenck, Jr. 4. Photo: Murray Lemmon. U.S. Dept. of Agriculture. 5. Photo: Lautman.   318–319 1. Naval Photographic Center, Washington, D.C. 2. Dept. of Transportation. 3,4. NASA Photo. 5. Photo: John F. Schleich. Naval Photographic Center, Washington, D.C.   320–321 1. Photo: Post-Wolcott, May 1941. LC. 2. Courtesy, *The Meadow Stud,* 1973. 3,4. VSCC.   322–323 1. 20th Cent.-Fox. 2. Courtesy, McFadden, Strauss and Irwin, Inc. 3. Courtesy, Jim Mahoney and Associates. 4. VSCC. 5. Courtesy, *The Daily Press, Inc.,* Newport News. 6. Courtesy, Audrey P. Franklyn, Los Angeles. 7. Courtesy, John Springer Associates, Inc. 8. Courtesy, *The Daily Press, Inc.,* Newport News. 9. Courtesy, Greenbrier Hotel, White Sulphur Springs.   324–325 1,2. Barter Theatre. 3. Wolf Trap Farm for the Performing Arts. 4. Photo: Patrick Gainer, April 1972. 5. Virginia Museum of Fine Arts. 6. Courtesy, The Mariner's Museum, Newport News.   326–327 1,7. VDCD. 2,6. Virginia State Board of Education. 3. Photo: C. Aubrey Bodine, Baltimore. 4. Photo: Saxer. Virginia Tech. 5. Photo: D'Adamo. VSCC.   328–329 1,2. Photo: Bea Kopp. *The Daily Press, Inc.,* Newport News, January 17, 1970. 3. *The New York Times,* September 1, 1970. 4. Photo: Willard Owens. *The Daily Press, Inc.,* Newport News, September 7, 1971. 5. Photo: Willard Owens. *The Daily Press, Inc.,* Newport News, August 12, 1971. 6. State Department of Education. Courtesy, Harry Smith. 330–331 1. Photo: courtesy, Janet Jenkins, Hotel Roanoke. 2. VDCD. 3. Photo: Phil Flournoy. VSCC. 4. Photo: *Richmond Times-Dispatch,* 1956. 5. Cartoon by Fred Seibel, 1949. University of Virginia Library, Manuscripts dept. 6. Cartoon by Fred Seibel, 1950. University of Virginia Library, Manuscripts dept.   332–333 1,4–6. Photo: Phil Flournoy. VSCC. 2. Photo: Wyman Viall, 1953. 3. Richmond Chamber of Commerce. 7. CSS. 334–335 1,2,4–6. Photo: Phil Flournoy. VSCC. 3. VSCC. 336–337 1. Photo: A. Aubrey Bodine. VHS. 2. Photo: Phil Flournoy. VSCC.   338–339 1,3. Photo: Phil Flournoy. VSCC. 2. Photo: Thomas L. Williams. CW. 4. CW. 5. U.S. Army Photo. 6. Photo: Dan Weiner. CW.

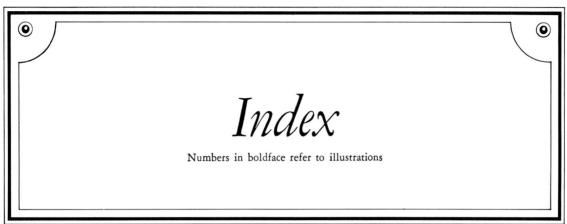

Index

Numbers in boldface refer to illustrations

ABC Buch (Henkel), **102**
Abingdon, 120, **121**, 300, 325
Abolitionism, 12, 13, 117, 119
Academies. *See* Education
Accomac, 136, 205
Act of Union (1707), 5
Adams, Henry, 217
Adams, John, 9, 11, 76, 93
Adams, John Quincy, 11
Advertisements
    by colonial merchants, **53**
    for fugitive slaves, **56, 57**
    for household remedies, **71**
    lottery (1615), **31**
    for peanuts, **245**
    for racing sires, **100, 101**
    for railroad, **130**
    revealing aspects of nineteenth-century life, 108, **109**
    for Richmond Academy, **86**
    for Richmond Locomotive and Machine Works, **236**
    for ship sailings, **69**
    for Straight Cut No. 1 (cigarettes), **240, 241**
Afton, 126
Age of Reason, 6
Aircraft carriers, **310**, 319
Airplanes, 288, **289**
Albany, N.Y., 7
Albemarle County, 64, 91, 135, 257
Album of Virginia (Beyer), 126, 129
Alderman, Edwin A., **295**
Alexander, James, 95
Alexandria, 5, 11, 16, 17, 95, 98, 101, 110, 119, 327
    federal troops in, **162, 163**
    growth of, **120–21**
    Unionists searching wagon near, **182**, 183
Algonquian Indians, **26**, 32
Alien and Sedition Acts of 1798, 11
Allan, John, 12
Allegheny Mountains, 8
Allen, Arthur, 39
Allen, Mrs. Willie, **257**
Allen family, **250–51**
Allen and Ginter (company), 240
Almond, J. Lindsay, Jr., 330
Ambler family, 56, **261**

Ambler plantation house, **261**
Amelia County, 78
American Indians. *See* Indians
American Revolution, 6, 8–10, 14, 53, 56, 59, 63, 64, 72–85, 95, 276, 307
    beginnings of, 72–73
    independence documents, 76–77
    leaders in, 74–75, 78–79, 147
    in the Piedmont and west, 78–79
    at sea, 80–81
    surrender at Yorktown, 10, 17, 80, **82–83, 84–85, 104, 105**, 228, 307
    Washington as commander in chief, 9, 67, 77, 78, **82–83, 84–85**, 89
"American of Virginia, An. Age 23" (Hollar), 26, **27**
Amish, 7
Anderson, Sherwood, 296, **297**
Anglicans, 4, 6, 7, 138
Annapolis, Md., 125
Anne, Queen, 5
Anti-lynch law, 283
Anti-organization Democrats, 298–99, 330
Apollo Room (Raleigh Tavern), **75**
Apothecary shop, **71**
Appalachian Mountains, 12, 63, 102, 333
Appalachian Trail, 302
Apple farming, 334, **335**
Appomattox Courthouse, 198, 211, 307
    Lee's surrender at, 14–15, 144, 191, 198–99, **200–201**
    Union troops at, **198**, 199
Appomattox River, 120, **190–91**
Aquia Creek, 162
Architecture, 6, 11, 39, 53, 86, 91, 108
Aristocracy, planter, 4, 5, 15, 58–59, 68–69
Aristotle, 6
Arlington, freedmen's village near, **183**
Arlington House, **143**, 338
Arlington National Cemetery, 338
Armaments, Civil War, 13, **152, 153, 177**

Armstrong, General Samuel, 16, **231**, 258–59
Army of Northern Virginia, 14, 191, 199, 202
    surrender of, 14–15, **144**, 198–99, **200–201**
Army of the Potomac, **151, 158**, 171, 183
Arnold, Benedict, 10, 78
Arthur, Chester, **228**
Articles of Confederation, 77
Arts, 5, 6, 12, 16–17, **274–75**, 296–97, **324–25**
Ash Lawn, **104**
Ashby, General Turner, 14, 174, **175**
Ashe, Arthur, 322, **323**
Ashland, 112
Ashmolean Museum (Oxford University), 27
Assateague Beach, **20, 21**
Assateague Pony Roundup, **336, 337**
Association for the Preservation of Virginia Antiquities (APVA), 17, 226, 261
Astor, Lady (Nancy Langhorne), 293
Astronauts, 319
"At the Market, Richmond" (Sheppard), **212–13**
Auction, tobacco. *See* Tobacco
Augusta County, 12, 102, 110, 112
Authentic and Impartial Narrative, An, 116, 117
Automobiles, 281, 300
    early, **272, 273, 284–85**
Award of Merit (fraktur drawing), 102, **103**
Aztec Indians, 3

Bacon, Nathaniel, 4, 42
Bacon's Castle, **38, 39**
Bacon's Rebellion of 1676, 4, 42
Bailey, Pearl, 17, **322**
Ballroom (Governor's Palace), 46, **47**
Ball's Bluff, battle of, **152**
Baltimore, Md., 15
Baltimore and Ohio Railroad, 15, 173
Banister, John, 6

Bank of Virginia, 147
Banners, for cigarettes, **243**
Baptisms, outdoor, 220–21
Baptist Church (Thumb Run), **267**
Baptists, 7, 12, 16, 138
Barber ship, 133
Barron, James and Richard, 10
Barter Theatre, **324, 325**
Bartlett, 300
Bath Alum Springs, **128**, 129
Bath County, 129
Bath house, 71
Battle, John S., **330**
Beatty, Warren, 322, **323**
"Behold, Virginia gives the fifth Kingdom" (motto), 5
Bellona Arsenal, **104–5**
Belmont Cup, 320
Berkeley, Governor Sir William, 4, 42, 43
Bernhart, Peter, 102
Berryman family, 250
Berryman house, **250**
Berryville, 302
Beveridge, Edythe, 275
Beyer, Edward, 126, 129, 133
Big Bethel, 158
Big Lick (Roanoke), 8, 225
Big Meadows, 302
Big Stone Gap, 296, 328
Bijou Theatre, 272
Bill of fare (Spotswood Hotel), **234, 235**
Bill of Rights, 10
Birth certificates, 102, **103**
Blackbeard, 51, 56, **57**
Blacks, 16, 235
    in American Revolution, 10
    in cigarette factories, 243
    education, 16, 218, 222–23, 231
    farm life, **218**
    growing role of, 17
    integration, 328–29, **330, 331**
    Johnston photos of, **268, 269**
    medical care of, 218
    nurse, 206
    in Reconstruction, 202, **203**, 206–7
    religion of, 218–19, 220–21
    suffrage for, 15
    voter registration, 206, **207, 222**
    See also Slaves and slavery
Blacksburg, 64
Blair, Reverend James, 4, 42, 43
Blair, James, II, 10
Bland, Richard, 6
Blimps, 288, **289**
    Roma tragedy, 290, **291**
Blow, Major William, 249
Blow family, 249
Blue Ridge Mountains, 7, 12, 24, 126
    springs area, **224**, 225
Blue Ridge Parkway, 24
Blyth, David Gilmour, 165
Boatwright, Frederic W., 295
Bonds (Civil War), 177
Bonhomme Richard (ship), 10
Boone, Daniel, 3, 8, **62, 63**, 226
Booth, Frances, **250**

Bootleg distilleries, **282**, 283
Boston, 9, 12, 16, 17, 317
Botetourt, Lord, 45
Bowden, Lemuel, **173**
Boyd, Belle, **174**
Boydton, 12, 112
Braddock, General Edward, 8
Brady, Mathew, 155, 191
    darkroom, 190, **191**
    photos of, 190–91, **199**
Brandon, 101
Brenneman, Peter, 102
Bridenbaugh, Carl, 8
Bridger, Jim, 3, **217**
Bridges, 281, 293, 314–15, 317
    covered, 225, **285**
    railroad, 165, 170, **171, 182**, 183
    swinging, 266–67
Bristol, **224**, 225
Broad Street (Richmond), 101, 146, 147, 192–93, 272, **273**, 276
Brockenbrough, Dr. John, 147
Brooke, Richard N., 218
Brown, John, **140**
    execution of, **141**
    raid at Harper's Ferry, 10, 13, 140–41
    trial, 140, **141**
Bruce, Philip Alexander, **305**
Brunswick County, 330
Bruton Parish Church, 44, **50, 51**, 231, 261, 308, 313, 338, **339**
    governor's pew, **50, 51**
Buck, Pearl, 296, **297**
Buena Vista, 15
Bugg's Island Dam, 300, **301**
Bull Run, first battle of, 14, **152**
Bull Run, second battle of, 165
Bullocks, 245
Bureau of American Ethnology, 217
"Burial of Latane, The," 174, **175**, 250, **251**
Burnside, General Ambrose, 173
Burr, Aaron, 11
Burwell family, 5
Butler, General Benjamin "Beast," 151, 185
    headquarters, 186, **187**
Butterbeans, harvesting, 334, **335**
Byrd, Harry, Jr., 299
Byrd, Harry, Sr., 4, 16, 17, 283, **295**, 299, 302, **303**
Byrd, Richard E., 299
Byrd, Richard E., Jr., 3, 299
Byrd, William, I, 4
Byrd, William, II, 6, 7, **58, 59**
Byrd family, 18, 299
Byrd organization, 330
Byrd Street Depot (Richmond), 271

Cabell, James Branch, 16, 296, **297**
Cabell, Mrs. James Branch, 296, **297**
Cabell, Joseph Carrington, 6
Cahokia, battle of, 9
California, 29
Camden (N.C.), battle of, 8
Cameron, William, 15

Camp meeting, 220, **221**
Camp Stuart, **288**
Campbell, William, 10
Campbell County, 120
Camptown Races, 320, **321**
Canals, 12, 15, **225**, 226–27, 240
    Chesapeake and Ohio, 178, 179
    in Civil War, 178, 179, **185**
    James River System, 10, **130–31, 132, 133**, 174, **178**, 179, 197, 225
    life on, 210, **211**
    rebuilding of, 211
    between Richmond and Lynchburg, 210, **211**
Cape Charles, 31
Cape Henry, 30–31, 32, 144
Capitol building (Jamestown), 5, **34–35**
Capitol building (Richmond), **86–87, 108–9, 135**, 147, **197, 209**, 272, 273, **292, 293, 316, 317, 338**
    collapse of floor in, **209**
    during the Civil War, 147
    Jefferson design for, 86–87, 317
Capitol building (Williamsburg), 44–45, 46, 232
    Assembly chambers in, **48, 49**
Caroline County, 6
Carpenter, Scott, 319
Carr, Dabney, 9
Carrington, V., 257
Carter, Miss Betty, 115
Carter, Robert "King," 4, **58, 59**
Carter family, 53
Carter Seminary graduation, 114–15
Carter's Grove, 5, **52, 53**, 250, 338, 339
Cartoons
    effect of shipping embargo on tobacco, 97
    of Fred Seibel, 330, **331**
    John Bull caricatured in, 98, **99**
    of loyalist merchants, 72, **73**
    "Moving Day" in Richmond, 196, 197
Caruthers, William A., 13
Cary Street (Richmond), 240, 271
Casino grounds (Newport News), 290, **291**
Casualties (Civil War), 188, **189**
Catesby, Mark, 6
Cather, Willa, 296, **297**
Catlin, George, 107
Caverns, 126, **127**
Cedar Creek, battle of, 180–81
Centreville, 153
Chambers, Lenoir, 16
Chancellorsville, battle of, 166, **167**
Chandler, Julian Alvin Carrol, 295
Chanler, John Armstrong, 257
Channing, William Ellery, 11
Chapel, Lee's, **205**
Chapin, J. R., 201
Chapman, Conrad Wise, 160, **161**
Chapman, George, 3
Charles I, King, **30, 31**
Charles II, King, 4

Charles City, 4, 13, 59
Charles City County, 12, 135, 185
Charles Town (Charleston, W. Va.), 141
Charlotte County, 72
Charlottesville, 12, 17, 64, 104, 112, 126, 330
  Revolutionary War encampment at, 78–79
Chataigne's Directory, 236
Chesapeake Bay, 5, 6, 16, 31, 69, 80, 98, 125, 162, 235, 310, 334
Chesapeake Bay Bridge-Tunnel, 314, 315
Chesapeake and Ohio Canal, 178, 179
Chesapeake and Ohio Railroad, 16, 235, 236, 265
Chesapeake Dry Dock and Construction Company, 16
Chesterfield County, 104, 115, 185, 186, 276
Chickahominy River, 217
"Chief's Wife and Child" (White), 26, 27
Chimborazo Hill, 165
Christian, Asbury, 271
Christian, Emily, 216, 217
Christiansburg, 117
"Christmas in the South" (Sheppard), 216, 217
Chrysler Hall, 325
Church Hill (Richmond), 174
Churchill, Winston, 312, 313
Churchill, Mrs. Winston, 312, 313
Cigarettes, 239
  advertisement for, 240, 241
  manufacturing, 242–43
Cincinnati, 15
Cities, growth of, 16, 17, 120–23, 316–17, 333
City Point, Grant's supply depot at, 186, 187
Civil War, 13–15, 16, 108, 110, 112, 129, 133, 136, 140–201, 215, 218, 220, 236, 243, 245, 276, 305, 328
  armaments, 13, 152, 153, 177
  Ball's Bluff battle, 152
  blockades, 154–55
  Brady photos of, 190–91, 199
  Bull Run, first battle, 14, 152
  Bull Run, second battle, 165
  defense of Washington, D.C. 182–83
  fall of Petersburg, 14, 188–91, 192, 193
  fall of Richmond, 14, 188, 191, 192–93, 194–95, 196–97
  first attacks, 13, 148–49
  at Fredericksburg, 170, 171
  Grant's pursuit of Lee, 14, 184–85
  at Hampton Roads, 14, 149, 150–51, 155, 156–57
  Harper's Ferry raid, 10, 13, 140–41
  heroes and heroines of, 174–75
  on the homefront, 176–77

ironclads' battle, 14, 155, 156–57
  Jackson in, 14, 152, 166–67, 174, 263
  on James River, 186–87
  map of, 144–45, 184, 185
  McClellan's campaign, 14, 160–61
  North's use of Virginia resources, 168–69
  Peninsula campaigns, 14, 144, 151, 158–59, 162, 165, 166, 174
  preparation for, 142–43
  Reconstruction. See Reconstruction
  Richmond as Confederacy capital, 13, 15, 146–47
  in Shenandoah Valley, 178, 179, 180–81
  surrender at Appomattox, 14–15, 144, 198–99, 200–201
  Union advances, 162–63
  veteran reunions, 262–63, 307
  in western Virginia, 172–73
Clark, George Rogers, 3, 9, 78
Clark, William, 3
Clay, Henry, 12
Clayton, John, 6
Clifton Forge, 15
Clinch River, 8
Coat of arms (Virginia), 30, 31, 42
Coleman, Dr. Charles Washington, 250
Coleman, Mrs. Charles Washington, 260, 261
Coleman, Miss Elizabeth Beverley, 250, 251
Coleman, George Preston, 250
Coles, Elizabeth Carter (Mrs. George C. Marshall), 286, 287
Coliseum (Hampton), 317
Coliseum (Richmond), 316, 317
Colonial National Historical Park, 35
Colonial Theatre, 272, 273
Columbia, 130–31
Columbus, Christopher, 265
Commerce Cafe, 276, 277
Committee of Correspondence, 9
Committee of Safety (1776–77), 9
Commonwealth Club, 275
Community colleges, 17
Conestoga wagons, 8
Confederate Memorial Day, 263
Confederate White House, 146–47
Connecticut, 231
Constitutional Convention (1787), 10, 98
Continental Congress, 6, 9
  Randolph as president of, 74, 75
Cook, George, 206, 211, 255
Cook, Huestis, 206, 211, 220, 250, 255
Cooke, John Esten, 13, 16
Cooke family, 5
Coolidge, Calvin, 295, 302
Coolidge, Mrs. Calvin, 302
Cooper, Gordon, 319
Corcoran, W. W., 204, 205
Corn whiskey, 282, 283
Cornwallis, General Charles, 10, 80,

83, 84–85, 104, 105, 158, 228, 307
"Cornwallis Resigning his Sword at Yorktown" (silk imprint), 104, 105
Cotten, Joseph, 322
Cotton, 244, 245
Council Chamber (Williamsburg), 49
Country fiddlers, 300
Courthouse (Norfolk), 264–65
Courts, 282, 283
Covered bridges, 225, 285
Cowpens, battle of, 8, 87
Crater, battle of the, 188
Crawford, William H., 12
Crime, 282–83
Cromwell, Oliver, 4
Cromwellian period, 42
Cross Keys, battle of, 166, 167
Crowe, Eyre, 133
Culpeper, 183, 185
Culpeper County, 67
  map of, 66
Cumberland (ship), 155
Cumberland Gap, 12, 61, 62, 63, 226–27
  Union capture of, 173
Cumberland Mountains, 8, 63
Cumberland Valley, 61
Cuninghame and Sons warehouse, 86
Cunningham, Anne Pamela, 17, 89
Curing tobacco, 238–39, 334
Currier and Ives, 193
Custer, Captain George, 158, 201
Custis Frances Parke, 68, 69
Custis, George Washington Parke, 143
Custis, John, 6
Custis, Colonel John, IV, 69
Customs House (Norfolk), 264–65
Cymbeline (Shakespeare), 51
Cypress trees, 24

Dabney, Virginius, 16
Dabney family, 7
Dale, Governor Sir Thomas, 36, 37
Dan River, 240
Dan River Mills, 332–33
Danville, 17, 120, 122–23, 240, 310, 332–33
  Confederate government at, 197, 199, 202, 293
  Lady Astor's home in, 293
  train wreck of 1908, 290
Darden, Colgate, Jr., 328, 330
Davis, Jefferson, 15, 146, 147, 176, 177, 193, 202
  at Confederate White House, 146–47
  in prison, 202
  trial for treason, 206, 207
Davis, Mrs. Jefferson, 176, 177
Davis, Governor Westmoreland, 298
Deane, Silas, 10
DeBry, Theodore, 26
Declaration of Independence, 6, 9
  voting for, 76–77
  writing of, 6, 9, 76, 91

Declaration of Rights (1776), 9, **75**
Deer hunt, **26**
Deerskin cloak, **26, 27**
DeHart, Captain, 161
Delaware, 144
Delaware (ship), bowsprit of, **125**
Delftware tile, **35**
Delius, Frederick, 17
Democratic party, 11, 15, 93, 215, 298, 302, 330
Democratic-Republican party, 11, 12
Depression of the 1930s, 300–301, 325
Dickens, Charles, 135
Dillard, James Hardy, 295
Dining room (Mount Vernon), **89**
Dinwiddie, Governor Robert, 8, 14
Diomed (thoroughbred), **254, 255**
Dirigibles, 288, **289**
   Roma tragedy, 290, **291**
Disasters, 208–9, 211, 290–91
Discovery (ship), 3
Dismal Swamp, 24, 129, **226–27**
District of Columbia. *See* Washington, D.C.
Dockside markets (Norfolk), **124–25**
Donne, John, 3
Drake, Sir Francis, 29
Drake's Branch, 240
Draper's Meadows (Blacksburg), 64
Drayton, Michael, 3, 21
Drewry family, 250, **251**
Drewry's Bluffs, 185
Dry dock (Newport News), **265**
Dry dock (Portsmouth), **124–25**
Duck hunting, **26,** 129
Duke of Gloucester Street (Williamsburg), 5, 46, **232, 233,** 308
Dulles Airport, **318,** 319, 325
Dumfries, 285
Dummy gun (Civil War), 152, **153**
Dunkers, 7
Dunlop's flour mill, **281**
Dunmore, Lord John, 9, 74, 75
DuPont de Nemours Company (E. I.), **332, 333**
Durkin, John, 243
Dutch Gap
   Butler's headquarters at, 186, **187**
   canal through, 185
Dynasties, 4, 5, 15, 58–59, 68–69

East Franklin Street (Richmond), 305
Eastern Shore, **336–37**
Eastward Ho! (Chapman and Marston), 3
Economy
   of plantations, 4, **56–57**
   post–World War I, 302
   tobacco, 4, **40–41,** 243
Edinburg post office, **284**
Education, 17, 110–15, 284, 294–95
   of blacks, 16, 218, **222–23,** 231
   first school in Valley of Virginia, 64
   graduation day, **114–15**
   integrating, 328–29, **330, 331**

land-grant schools, 231
   leadership in, **112–13**
   post–World War II, **326–27**
   public schools, 15, 16, 215
   spread of, 12, **230–31**
Ege, Jacob, 135
Ege house, **134,** 135
Egyptian Building (Medical College of Virginia), **274, 275**
Eisenhower, Dwight, **312, 313**
Eisenhower, Mrs. Dwight, **312, 313**
Electric power, 300
Elizabeth I, Queen, 3, 29
Elizabeth II, Queen, **313**
Elizabeth, Queen Mother, **313**
Elizabeth River, **319**
Emancipation, 13, 183, 218
Emancipation Proclamation (1863), 16, 169, 206
"En dat Virginia Quintum" (motto), 5
End of the Hunt, The, **54–55**
Enterprise (carrier), **310**
Entertainers, 17, 51, **322–23**
Entrance gate (Governor's Palace), **46, 47**
Episcopal High School (Alexandria), **326,** 327
Episcopal Memorial Church (Richmond), **138**
Episcopalians, **98,** 138
Equal Suffrage League, **292, 293**
Erie Canal, 12
"Evacuation of Richmond, The . . . by the Government of the Southern Confederacy" (Currier and Ives), **192–93**
Ewell, Richard S., 14
Exchange Hotel **108, 134, 135**
Excursion boats, **136–37, 228**

Fairfax County, 75, 314, 327
Fairfax family, 67
Fairfax Resolves, 75
Fairs, **268**
Falmouth, 5, 7, 11
Family life, **102, 250–51**
Farmers' Bank of Richmond, **133**
Farms, 10, 17, **244–47, 334–35**
   life of blacks on, **218**
   at Marion, **20, 21**
   nineteenth-century revolution in, 130–31
   in Valley of Virginia at spring plowing time, 21, **22–23**
   See also Plantations; Tobacco
Fauquier, Governor Francis, 6, 44, **45**
Fauquier County, 67, 267
   map of, **66, 67**
Federal Reserve System, 17
Federalist party, 93
Ferry farm, 120
Field cap (Civil War), **166**
Field desk, Washington's, **67**
Field hospital (Civil War), **161**
Fielding, Henry, 4, 55
Fifteenth Amendment, 15
Filene Center, **324, 325**

Fincastle, 17
First Baptist Church (Richmond), 138, **139**
First Continental Congress, 9
First Presbyterian Church (Staunton), 138, **139**
First Virginia Regiment, 257
Fishing, **234–35, 281, 300, 334, 335**
Fitzgerald, Ella, 17, **322, 323**
Five Indian Nations, 7
"Flapper era," 257, **293**
Flintlock rifle (Civil War), 152, **153**
Floods of 1870, **208–9**
Florida, 4
Fluvanna County, 130
"Flyer, The" (White), **26, 27**
Fontaine family, 7
Forbes, General John, 8
Ford, Henry, 16
Fort Bridger, 217
Fort Duquesne, 8
   map of, **67**
Fort Egypt, **60, 61**
Fort Eustis, **288**
Fort houses, **60, 61**
Fort Monroe, **98,** 129, 147, **149, 150, 151,** 158, **202**
   General Wool sailing from, **150,** 151
Fort Myer, **288**
Fort Norfolk, **125**
Fort Pickens, 144
Fort Sedgwick, **188**
Fort Sumter, 11, 13, 143
Fossil fuels, 333
Foundations
   of first state house, **34–35**
   of log houses, **60, 61**
Fourteenth Amendment, 15
Fox, John, Jr., 16, **296**
Fox hunting, **55, 255**
Fraktur drawings, 102, **103**
Francis Street (Williamsburg), 5
Francisco, Peter, **78**
Frank Leslie's Illustrated Newspaper, 151, 166, 167, 170, 171, **193, 194–95, 220, 221**
   See also Picture Credits
Franklin, Benjamin, 10
Franklin Street (Richmond), **262–63**
Fredericksburg, 5, 7, 53, 95, 117, 120, 165
   battle for, **170, 171**
   railroads, 15
Freedmen, **183, 197**
Freedmen's Bureau, 16
Freeman, Douglas Southall, 16, 305
French and Indian Wars, 8
   Washington in, 8, **66, 67**
Friendship Fire House (Alexandria), **95**
Fry, Joshua, 8, 56
Fry-Jefferson Map of Virginia (1751), 8, **56**

Gadsby's Tavern, **95**
Gaines, Francis Pendleton, 295

Gaines's Mill, battle of, 161
Galt, Miss Mary, 260, 261
Gamble's Hill (Richmond), 132, 133
Gaol (Williamsburg), 51
"General Sigel's [Union] Corps at the Second Battle of Bull Run," 165
Generall Historie of Virginia, New England and the Sumner Isles (Smith), 26, 31, 32
  illustrations of adventures (1607–9), 26, 32–33
George III, King, 6
Georgia, 8, 12
Georgian architecture, 53
German Baptists, 7
German immigrants, 7, 8, 24, 61, 91, 97, 296
  drawings of, 102, 103
  in the Revolutionary War, 8
Gettysburg, battle of, 174
Gibson, Charles Dana, 257
Gibson, Mrs. Charles Dana, 256, 257
"Gibson Girl, The," 257
Giles County, 267
Ginter, Major Lewis, 240
Ginter Park (Richmond), 240
"Give me liberty or give me death" speech, 72
Glasgow, Ellen, 16, 296, 297, 327
Glasgow house, 327
Glass, Carter, 17, 298, 299
Glenn, John, 319
Glorious Revolution of 1688, 4, 9
Gloucester, 42, 80, 275, 314
  bridge between Yorktown and, 314
Gloucester County, 253, 338
Godspeed (ship), 3
Godwin, Governor Mills E., Jr., 328, 330
Golf, 322
Gooch, Governor William, 7
Goochland County, 7, 250
Goodwin, Reverend William A. R., 260, 261, 308, 312, 313
Gordonsville, 235
Gosport (Portsmouth), 69
Governor's Mansion (Richmond), 135, 214, 215, 330–31
Governor's Office (Richmond), 330
Governor's Palace (Williamsburg), 46, 47
  bodies of Revolutionary soldiers at, 306, 307
Grace Street (Richmond), 275
Graduation day, 114–15
Graduation program, 114
Graham, Reverend William, 64
Grammar and Matty School, 230, 231
Grand Caverns, 126, 127
Grant, Ulysses S., 15, 183, 184, 185, 199, 201
  battle for Petersburg, 14, 188–89
  James River campaign, 186–87
  pursuit of Lee, 14, 184–85
Grasse, Marquis François de, 80

Graves, Admiral Thomas, 80
Great Bridge, battle of, 9
Great Charter of Privileges, Orders, and Laws, 3–4, 37
Great Lakes, 12
Great Wagon Road, 8, 12, 61, 117
Greek chorus, 258, 259
Grissom, Virgil "Gus," 319
Guilford Courthouse, battle of, 8
Gulf of Mexico, 7
Gum Springs, 322
Gunston Hall, 75, 95
Gwynn's Island, battle of, 9

Halifax, 330
Hallan, Nancy, 51
Hallowell, Benjamin, 110
Hallowell school, 110
Hamilton, Alexander, 11, 82–83, 93
Hamilton, Governor Sir Henry, 9, 51
Hamlet (Shakespeare), 258–59
Hampden-Sydney College, 12, 64, 138
Hampton, Wade, 13, 205
Hampton, 5, 14, 16, 98, 110, 288, 290, 319
  aerial view of, 316, 317
  burning of, 151
Hampton Creek, 151
Hampton Institute, 16, 17, 222, 223, 231
  1875 graduating class, 258–59
Hampton Roads, 14, 149, 150–51, 310, 311, 333
  aerial view of, 316, 317
  bridge-tunnel across, 314, 315, 317
  International Naval Rendezvous at (1893), 264–65
  ironclads' battle at, 149, 155, 156–57
  Jamestown Exposition of 1907 at, 278–79
  during World War I, 288–89
Hampton Roads (steamer), 281
Handbills, 173, 192
Handy, May, 257
Hanover County, 12, 72, 206, 236, 276, 320
Harper's Ferry
  arsenal at, 140, 141, 148, 149
  John Brown's raid at, 10, 13, 140–41
  railroads, 15
Harper's Weekly, 136, 144–45, 154, 155, 165, 198, 199, 212–13, 243
  See also Picture Credits
Harrison, Albertis, Jr., 330
Harrison, Benjamin, 10
Harrison, Benjamin, II, 4
Harrison, Nathaniel, 101
Harrison, William Henry, 9, 12
Harrisonburg, 327
Harvard University, 11
Hatcher, Robert V., 313
Hayes, Helen, 324, 325
Health care, 70–71
  of blacks, 218

Henkel, Andrew, 102
Henrico County, 42, 276
Henrico Parish Church (St. John's Church), 72
Henry, John, 63, 67
  map by (1770), 66, 67
Henry, Patrick, 6, 9, 10, 72
  law office of, 72
Henry, 330
Herndon, 300
Hessian soldiers, 78
Highways, 17, 314–15
Hill, General Ambrose P., 14
Hill, General Daniel Harvey, 14
Hill family, 5, 53
Historical and Industrial Guide to Petersburg (Pollock), 245
Historical and Pictorial Essay (Tatham), 96, 97
Historical Collections of Virginia (Howe), 117
History, study of, 304–5
Hite, Joist, 7
Hoge, Reverend Moses, 138
Hogs, slaughtering, 235, 244, 245
Hollar, Wenceslaus, 26
Hollin Hills School, 326, 327
Holston River, 8
Holton, Governor Linwood, 320
  inauguration, 328
Hoover, Herbert, 306, 307
Hoover, Mrs. Herbert, 306, 307
Horse-and-carriage transportation, 273
Horses
  advertisement for sires, 100, 101
  automobile's displacement of, 284
  jumping, 255
  racing, 53, 254–55, 320–21
  See also names of horses
Hospitals, 168–69
  field (Civil War), 161
  rates, 177
Hot Springs, 322
Houdon, Jean Antoine, 338
House of Burgesses, 6
  chamber in Williamsburg, 48
  See also Virginia Assembly
House of Commons, 37
House of Delegates, 86, 299, 313
Household items (seventeenth century), 34–35
Household remedies, 71
Houston, Sam, 3, 12
Howard of Effingham, Lord, 7
Howe, Henry, 117, 125
Howe's *Historical Collections of Virginia,* 120, 121
Howlett's Confederate battery, 186, 187
Hoxton House (Alexandria Episcopal High School), 326, 327
Hudson Valley, 16
Huguenots, 7
Hunt, Reverend Robert, 3
Hunting, 5, 26, 55, 100, 101, 129, 255
Huntington, Archer and Anna Hyatt, 325

Huntington, Collis P., 16, **265**
Hyde, Benjamin, 53
Hygeia Hotel, **150**
  McClellan's army at, **151**

Ice wagon, 276, **277**
Illinois, 5, 9, 12
Illustrated London News, The, 152, 171
  See also Picture Credits
Inca Indians, 3
Independence Hall, 76
Indiana, 9
Indian-Negro family, **217**
Indians, 3, 7, 8, 24, 26–27, 31, 32, 222, 298
  early encounters with, 36–37
  massacre of 1622, 42
  medals given to, 37
  peace treaty with (1677), 37
  slaughters in Kentucky, 63
Industry
  in 1800s, 130–33
  post-World War I, 16
  present-day, 17, 332–33
Inflation, 177
Ingles, William, 61
Ingles ferry and tavern, **60–61**
Integration, 328–29
  political cartoon about, 330, **331**
Intellectual life, in Richmond, 134–35
International Lagoon (Jamestown Exposition of 1907), 278–79
International Naval Rendezvous (1893), **264–65**
Interstate Highway System, 314, 317
Ireland Street (Williamsburg), 5
Iroquois Indians, 7
Isle of Wight County, 293
Italian-style architecture, 91
Ivanhoe (Scott), 13

Jackson, Andrew, 12
Jackson, General Thomas Jonathan "Stonewall," 14, 152, **166–67,** 174, **263**
Jacksonville, Fla., 271
Jails, 51
James I, King, 30, **31**
James City, 4
James River, 4, 5, 6, 7, 10, 11, 12, 17, 35, 39, 44, 53, 86, 108, 120, 136, 162, **165, 184,** 185, 225, 235, 239, 240, 245, 250, 271, 288, 293, 333
  blockade of (1862), 155
  boat races on, **281**
  Confederate defense of, 186, **187**
  evacuation of Richmond across, 192–93
  flood of 1870, **208–9**
  Union command post on, **186**
James River Canal System, 10, 130–31, **132, 133,** 174, **178, 179,** 197, **225**
Jamestown, 3, 11, 12, 30–35, 69, 239, 268
  excavations at, 34–35, **308**

first Assembly meeting at, 4, **36,** 37, 39
founding of, 3, 30–31
historic celebrations, 17, **136–37,** **278–79,** 307
Jamestown church, 39, 226, **227, 261**
Jamestown Exposition of 1907, 278–79
Jamestown Festival Park, **313**
Jamestown Island, 261
Jamestown Visitor Center (Colonial National Historical Park), 35
Janney, Amos, 61
Janney's Mill, 60, **61**
Jaquelin, Elizabeth, **68, 69**
Jasper, John, 222
Jean and Virginia (yacht), **250**
Jefferson, Peter, 8, 56
Jefferson, Thomas, 3, 9, 10, 11–12, 13, 17, 18, 44, 74, 75, **90,** 93, **253**
  background of, 6
  capitol designed by, 86–87, **317**
  embargo against British, 97, 98
  home of, 10, **90–91**
  writing of Declaration of Independence, 6, 9, 76, 91
Jefferson, Thomas Garland, **179**
Jennings, Frank, **284**
Jewell Ridge Coal Mine, 332–33
Johnson, Andrew, 15
Johnston, Frances Benjamin, 268
  photographs by, **268, 269**
Johnston, General Joseph E., 14, **158,** 205
Johnston, Mary, 16, **296**
Jones, John Paul, 10
Jonesville, 217
Jouett, Jack, 10
Jousting tournament, **255**
Joux, Reverend Benjamin de, 7
Jury, blacks on, 206, **207**

Kanawha River, 10
Kashaskia, battle of, 9
Kenilworth (Scott), 13
Kenmore (home), 53
Kennedy High School (Richmond), 328
Kentucky, 3, 8, 11, 12, 63, 112, 226, 236
Kentucky rifles, 8
Kilgore house, 60, **61**
King's Mountain, battle of, 8
Kiptopeke, 314
Kirmess ball, 257
Kitchen (Mount Vernon), **89**
Kitchen utensils, 34, **35**
Knox, John, 7, **82–83**

Lafayette, James, **83**
Lafayette, Marquis de, **82–83**
  death of, 104
  return to Virginia (1824), 104, **105**
Lafayette, Mlle. Virginia, 104
Lake Anne Village Center (Reston), 317

Lake Drummond Hotel, **129**
Lake Erie, 67
Lancaster, Treaty of (1744), 7
Lancaster County, 4, 59
Land-grant schools, 231
Langhorne, Irene, **256, 257**
Langhorne, Nancy (Lady Astor), 293
Langley Field, 290, 319
Latané family, 7
Latrobe, Benjamin, 83, 89, 117
Law office (Patrick Henry), **72**
Leadership
  colonial, 42–43
  in education, 112–13
  during the Revolution, 74–75, 78–79, 147
Lee, Arthur, 10
Lee, Fitzhugh, 16, **214, 215,** 270, 271
Lee, George Washington Custis, **205**
Lee, Henry "Lighthorse Harry," 6, 9, 10
Lee, Richard Henry, 6, 9
Lee, Robert E., 13–14, 16, 17, 18, 110, 112, **140, 141, 143, 158,** 166, 174, **199, 201, 204, 205,** 271, **275,** 305, 307, 338
  death of, 205, 208
  evacuation of Richmond, 14, 191, 193
  fall of Petersburg, 14, 188, **189,** 191, 193
  farewell to troops, 14–15, **199**
  Grant's pursuit of, 14, 184–85
  statues of, 205, 262, **263, 275**
  surrender at Appomattox, 14–15, 144, 191, 198–99, **200–201**
  on Traveller, **164, 165**
  as Washington College president, 165, 204, **205**
Lee, Mrs. Robert E., **204,** 205
Lee, Thomas, 4, **58, 59**
Lee County, 217
Lee family, 104
Letcher, Governor John, **142, 143,** 231
Letcher family, 7
Leviathan (ship), 302, **303**
Lewis, General Andrew, 9
Lewis, Fielding, 53
Lewis, Meriwether, 3
Lexington, 24, 112, 126, 130, 143, 165, 205, 287, 295, 299
Libby Prison, **164, 165**
"Liberation Day," 206, **207**
Liberty Hall (college), **64**
"Liberty Launching Day" (1918), **288**
Light Infantry Blues (militia group), 271
Lincoln, Abraham, 13, 14, 16, 143, 161, 169, 206
  in Richmond, **197**
Linton, Henry, 226
Literature, 12–13, 16, 135, 296–97
Little Bethel, battle at, 151
Little Colonel, The (motion picture), **322**
Little Creek, 151

Little Sorrel (horse), 263
Locke, John, 6, 9
Log houses, 60, 61, 97, 112, 218
Lottery advertisement of 1615 (Virginia Company), 31
Loudoun County, 152
Louis XIV, King, 7
Louisa County, 10
Louisiana Territory, 3, 11
Lower class, 216–17
Loyalist merchants, cartoon of, 72, 73
Ludwell, Philip, I, 4
Ludwell-Paradise House, 308
Lunatic Asylum (Williamsburg), 70, 71, 232, 233
Luray, 61
Lutherans, 8
Luxury, eighteenth century, 52–55
Lynchburg, 11, 17, 120, 121, 126, 179, 225, 240, 298, 305
    canal between Richmond and, 210, 211
Lynching, 283
Lynch's Ferry, 120

MacArthur Memorial, 313
McClellan, General George B., 151, 158, 161, 162
    Richmond campaign, 14, 160–61
McClurg, Dr. James, 10, 70, 71
McCormick, Cyrus, 12, 130
    inventions of 130, 131
    workshop, 130, 131
McCrea, Mr. and Mrs. Archibald, 338, 339
McDowell, Dr. Ephraim, 70, 71
McGuffey, William Holmes, 112
McGuffey's Readers, 112
Machodoc Indians, 37
MacLaine, Shirley, 322, 323
McLean residence, 198, 199, 201
McMurran, Lewis, 313
Madison, Dolley, 98
Madison, James, 6, 10, 11, 12, 17, 93, 98
    marriage of, 98
    as president, 98
    at Virginia Constitutional Convention (1828–30), 106–7
Madison, Reverend James, 98
Madison College, 327
Magazine (Williamsburg), 9, 46, 260, 261
Magruder, Colonel John B., 151
Mahone, General William, 15, 16, 188, 214, 215
Main Street (Richmond), 133, 192–93, 194–95, 196, 197, 206, 207, 211, 243, 276
Maison Carrée (Nimes), 86
Malone, Dumas, 6
Manassas, Confederate quarters near, 165
Manchester (South Richmond), 133
Mandolin club, 258, 259
Mann, Governor William Hodges, 287

Maphis, John, 102
Maps
    battle of Virginia Capes (1781), 80, 81
    Civil War, 144–45, 184, 185
    Culpeper County, 66, 67
    dividing line with North Carolina, 58
    Fauquier County, 66, 67
    Fort Duquesne, 67
    by Fry-Jefferson (1751), 8, 56
    by John Henry (1770), 66, 67
    by John Smith, 33
    Middle Plantation, 44
    "New and Accurate Map of Virginia" (1770), 62, 63
    railroad (1832), 130
    "Sea of China and the Indies, The" (1651), 28, 29
    tobacco farms and plantations (1681), 40
    Virginia (1880), xii–xiii
    Washington, D.C., 92–93
    Washington's land holdings, 88, 89
Mariner's Museum (Newport News), 325
Marion, 296
    farm at, 20, 21
Markets, 124–25, 206, 211, 212–13, 225, 276, 277
    tobacco, 239, 240, 241, 334
Marshall, George C., 286, 287
Marshall, Mrs. George C. (Elizabeth Carter Coles), 286, 287
Marshall, John, 6, 10, 11, 12, 13, 93, 119
    at Virginia Constitutional Convention (1828–30), 106–7
Marshall, Thomas, 298, 299
Marshall Museum and Library, 287
Marston, John, 3
Mary II, Queen, 4
Mary Baldwin College, 327
Mary of Norfolk (pilot vessel), 124, 125
Maryland, 7, 11, 14, 17, 29, 93, 144, 173, 180, 337
    population (1685), 4
Mason, George, 9, 10, 13, 74, 75
Massachusetts, 93
    first settlement of, 4
    population (1685), 4
Massachusetts Institute of Technology, 110
Massey, Reverend J. E., 214, 215
Mathews County, 267
Mattaponi Indians, 298
Maupin, Socrates, 112
Maury, Matthew Fontaine, 231
Maury family, 7
Mayo's Bridge, 133
Mayo's Island, 281
Mays, David, 16
Meade, General George, 183, 185
Meade, Bishop William, 138
Mecklenburg County, 300
Medals, for Indians, 37

Medical College of Virginia, 12, 101, 275
    hospital rates, 177
Mennonites, 7, 102
Mental hospital, 70, 71, 232, 233
Mercer, Hugh, 71
Mercer's apothecary shop, 71
Merrimack (ironclad), 14, 155
    burning of, 149
    See also Virginia
Methodists, 12, 16, 112, 138
Mexican War, 14
Michaux, Dr. Jacob, 274, 275
Michel, Francis Louis, 44
Michie's Tavern, 64, 65
Michigan, 9
Middle Ages, 5
Middle class, 216–17
Middle Plantation. See Williamsburg
Miley, Michael, 165, 205
Military commission, 143
Miller, Francis Pickens, 330
Miller, Lewis, 117
Mills, 60, 61, 267
Mineral springs, 128–29
Mining, 332–333
Minor, John B., 112
Mississippi, 147
Mississippi River, 7
Mississippi Valley, 7, 12
Missouri Compromise, 11–12
Model-T Ford, 16, 285
Monacan Indians, 7
Moncure family, 7
Money
    issued by Virginia, 75
    tobacco warehouse receipts as, 56
Monitor (ironclad), 14, 149, 155, 156–57
    crew of, 155
Monkey (racing sire), 100
Monroe, James, 6, 10, 11, 12, 13, 93, 98, 104, 119, 330
    law office of, 95
    at Virginia Constitutional Convention (1828–30), 106–7
Montesquieu, Baron de, 6
Montgomery, Ala., 13, 147
Montgomery County, 117, 129
Monticello, 10, 90–91
    sketch of, 91
    west front of, 90, 91
Montpelier, 6
Monumental Episcopal Church, 101
Mooney, James, 217
Moore, Augustine, 83
Moore, Bishop Richard Channing, 138
Moore house, 83
Morecock, Miss Pinky, 258, 259
Morgan, Daniel, 10, 78, 79
Mosby, Colonel John Singleton, 14, 174, 175, 179
Mossy Creek Academy, 110
Moton, Robert, 17
Motto (Virginia), 5
Mount Pleasant (house), 5
Mount Vernon, 17, 88, 95, 118, 119, 327

Mount Vernon (*Continued*)
dining room, **89**
folk painting resembling, **68–69**
map of, **88, 89**
Mount Vernon Ladies' Association of the Union, 89
Muhlenberg, Reverend John Peter, 8, 78
Mulberry Island, 288
Murder, 283
Murphy's Hotel, **273**

Nansemond, 330
Nashville, Tenn., 205
Nashville (ship), **270, 271**
Nassau Street (Williamsburg), 5
National Aeronautics and Space Administration (NASA), 319
National Park Service, 35, 126, 261
Natural Bridge, 24, 126, **226**
Naval Air Station (Norfolk), 288, **289**
Naval Hospital (Portsmouth), **125**
Navigation Act, 4
Negro Foot, 206
Nelson, General Thomas, Jr., 83
Nelson County, 12
Nelson family, 56
Nelson house, 83
Nelson-Galt house, **216, 217**
Neoclassical architecture, 11, 86, 108
"New and Accurate Map of Virginia" (1770), **62, 63**
New Deal, 16, 17
New Jersey, 17
New Kent County, 83
New Life of Virginea, The (broadside), 37
New Market, 102, 179
New Nolichucky River, 8
New River, **21,** 61
New York, 7, 9, 12, 14, 93, 191
population (1685), 4
New York Times, The, 328
Newport News, 15, 17, 155, 158, 271, 281, 283, 288, 290, 293, 302, 310, 322, 325, 333
aerial view of, **316, 317**
anti-integration pickets in, 328, 329
dry dock at, **265**
Newport News Shipbuilding and Dry Dock Company, 271
Newport Parish Church (St. Luke's Church), 17, **38, 39**
Nicholson, Mrs. Bailey, **300**
Nicholson, Governor Francis, 5, 7
Nicholson Street (Williamsburg), 5
Nineteenth Amendment, 293
Ninth Congressional District, 302
Ninth Street (Richmond), 276
Non-Organization Democrats, 298–99, 330
Norfolk, 5, 9, 10, 11, 14, 16, 17, 39, 101, 151, 226, 232, 261, 271, 278, 281, 288, 290, 313, 314, 317, 325, 330
aerial view of, **316, 317**
dockside markets, **124–25**

federal occupation of, **154, 155**
as harbor, **124–25, 264–65**
Norfolk Navy Yard, ruins of, **168–69**
Norfolk Symphony, 325
North Carolina, 3, 8, 9, 32, 63, 129, 144, 193, 226, 300, 302
dividing line with Virginia, **58**
North Mayo River, 285
North Pole, 3
North Sixth Street (Richmond), 276
Northwest Territory, 9, 78
Nova Britannia, 29

Oath of allegiance (1865), **202**
soldiers and officers signing, 202, **203**
Ocean View beach, **280, 281**
"Ode to the Virginian Voyage" (Drayton), 3
Ohio, 9, 12
Ohio River, 9, 78
Ohio Valley, 7, 8, 10, 12, 15, 63
settlement of, **8**
Virginia's cession of, 4
Old Dominion Line (steamer company), 281
Old Point, 16
Old Point Comfort, 147, 149
Old tower (1639 church), **39**
Orchards, **21, 334, 335**
Oregon Trail, 3, 217
Organ grinder, **276**
Organization Democrats, 298
Otter, Peaks of, **24, 25**
Oxford University, 27
Oyster shucking house, 234, **235**

Pagan River, 250
Page, John, 253
Page, Matthew, 42, 43
Page, Thomas Nelson, 17
Page family, 5
Palladio, Andrea, 91
Pamunkey Indians, 37, **298**
Pamunkey River, 162, **171**
Paris, Treaty of (1783), 10
Parke, Daniel, II, **58, 59**
Parrington, Vernon Louis, 6, 13
Paspahagh Indians, 32
Past, preserving, 260–61
Pasteur, William, 71
"Pastoral Visit, A" (Brooke), **218–19**
Peabody, George, 204, **205**
Peaks of Otter, **24, 25**
Peale, James, 83
Peanuts
advertisement for, **245**
picking, 245, **246–47**
Pen, for slaves, **119**
Pendleton, Edmund, 6
Peninsula campaign, 14, 144, 151, 158–59, 162, 165, 166, 174
Pennsylvania, 7, 14, 93, 119, 287
Pennsylvania Gazette, 69
Pennsylvania rifles, 8
Pennsylvania Statehouse (Independence Hall), 76

Pentagon, **318, 319**
Pericles, 6
Pershing, General John J., **306, 307**
Pétain, Marshal Henri, **306, 307**
Petersburg, 5, 7, 10, 11, 13, 15, 101, 120, 133, 185, 186, **189,** 215, 245, 322
Brady photos of, **190–91**
fall of, 14, 188–91, **192, 193**
railroads, 15
"Petersburg Express" (mounted cannon), 188, **189**
Petersburg High School, 191
Philadelphia, 9, 10, 16, 75, 98, 119, 228
Phillips, General, 10
"Picket Post" (Chapman), **160, 161**
Pickett, General George E., 174, **175**
Picturesque America (Linton), 226
Pierce-Arrow, **287**
Pierpont, Governor Francis, 15, 173
Pigs, slaughter of, 235, **244, 245**
Pine Beach, 278
Piracy, 56
Pittsburgh, 8, 67
Plantations, 83, 95, 174, 183
aristocracy, 4, 5, 15, 58–59, 68–69
economy, 4, 40–41, 56–57
folk painting of, **68–69**
life (eighteenth century), 56–57
slaves imported for, 56
tobacco, map of (1681), **40**
See also names of plantations
Planter's ledger, 56
Plaster mask wall decoration, 34, 35
Plato, 6
Playbills, **51, 101**
Pleasants, John Hampden, 11, 93
Plymouth, Mass., 12
Pocahontas, 3, **32**
Poe, Edgar Allan, 12–13, **135,** 226
Poe museum, **135**
Politics, 17, 134–35, 214–15, 298–99, 302–3, 330–31
Poll tax, 15
Pollard, Governor John Garland, **306, 307**
Pollock, Edward, 245
Pontoon causeway (Petersburg), 191
Population, Virginia, 4, 17
Port Royal, 5, 11
Porterfield, Robert, **324, 325**
Portsmouth, 69
aerial view of, **316, 317**
as harbor, **124–25**
shipyards at, 319
Portsmouth Navy Yard, **125**
destruction of (1861), **148–49**
Pory, John, 37
Potomac Baptist Association, **258, 259**
Potomac Creek, **182, 183**
Potomac Indians, 37
Potomac River, 4, 7, 11, 12, 89, **92–93,** 98, 130, 143, 179, 319
Confederate installation on, 162, 163
Union fort on, **183**
Pottery, 35

Powder Magazine (Williamsburg), 9, 46, 260, 261
Powell, John, 17, 296, 297
Powell, Lewis, Jr., 17
Powhatan, Chief, 26, 32, 33, 217
Presbyterian "log college," 64
Presbyterians, 12, 138, 287
Preston, Colonel William, 64
Price, Birch & Company, 119
Prince Edward County, 64, 158
Prince George County, 101
Prince Street (Alexandria), 94, 95
Princeton University, 64
Printing Office (Williamsburg), 232
Prissy (serving girl), 216, 217
Prohibition, 276, 283
Provisional Army of Virginia, 143
Public health care, 70–71
Public magazine (Williamsburg), 9, 46, 260, 261
Public schools. See Education
Public spring, 216–17
Pulitzer prize, 16
Pump primer, 300, 301
Purdie, Alexander, 72, 76
Puritans, 4

Quakers, 61, 110
Quesnay de Beaurepaire, 86

R. E. Lee (Freeman), 305
Radford, 61
Radical Republicans, 15, 215
Railroads, xii, 15, 16, 17, 179, 202, 209, 225, 235, 236–37, 265
  advertisement for, 130
  bridges, 165, 170, 171, 182, 183
  Danville wreck of 1908, 290
  depots, 191, 236, 237, 271
  rebuilding of, 211
  timetable, 236, 237
  Union control of B&O, 173
Railway Directory (C&O), 235
Raleigh, Sir Walter, 3, 29
Raleigh Tavern, 75, 104
"Ramble in Virginia, A" (magazine article), 225
Randolph, David Meade, 11
Randolph, Edmund, 6, 10, 11, 74, 75
Randolph, James Innes, 143
Randolph, John, 6
Randolph, John (of Roanoke), 12, 100, 101
  at Virginia Constitutional Convention (1828–30), 106–7
Randolph, Peyton, 6, 9
Randolph, William, 42, 43
Randolph family, 5
Randolph-Macon College, 12, 112, 113, 296
Raphine, 130
Rapists, 283
Rappahannock River, 120
Rascoe, Burton, 296, 297
Readjuster Convention (1881), 215
"Readjusters," 15, 215
Reaper, 130, 131

"Reconnaissance in force by Gen'l Gorman before Yorktown" (Homer), 158, 159
Reconstruction, 15–16, 17, 202–7, 236, 298
  politics of, 214–15
  revival of Richmond, 210–11
  role of blacks in, 202, 203, 206–7
Southern leaders' promotion of, 204, 205
Reconstruction Act of 1867, 15
Red Hill plantation, 72
Reed, Dr. Walter, 274, 275
  birthplace of, 338
Regimental band (Virginia Polytechnic Institute), 326, 327
Religion, 16, 138–39, 267
  of blacks, 218–19, 220–21
  See also names of churches; names of religious groups
Religious freedom, statute for, 91
Remedies, household, 71
Republican party, 11, 15, 16, 215, 298, 302, 328
Reston (planned community), 317
Restoration of Williamsburg, 17, 307, 308, 309
"Resurrection of Henry Box Brown, The," 119
Richmond, xii, 5, 7, 12, 13, 15, 17, 72, 83, 93, 101, 104, 119, 132–35, 158, 179, 186, 206, 218, 220, 236, 243, 245, 276–77, 305, 307, 313, 322, 325, 327, 328, 333, 338
  aerial view of, 316, 317
  British attack on (1781), 78, 79
  canal between Lynchburg and, 210, 211
  Civil War fighting near, 160, 161
  as Confederacy capital, 13, 15, 146–47
  Confederate reunions in, 262–63, 307
  fall of (1865), 14, 188, 191, 192–93, 194–95, 196–97
  under federal occupation, 202
  flood of 1870, 208–9
  industry, 132–33, 152–53, 177, 236, 332, 333
  Lee's headquarters in, 199
  Libby Prison, 164, 165
  morale during Civil War, 177
  political and intellectual life, 108–9, 134–35
  railroad depot, 191, 236, 237 271
  revival of, 210–11
  selection as state capital, 10, 11, 86–87
  statue of Lee in, 205, 262 263
  Unionist spy in, 174
Richmond Academy advertisement, 86
Richmond Daily Enquirer, 142, 143
Richmond and Danville Railroad, 197
Richmond Enquirer, 11, 93, 108
Richmond German (organization), 276, 277

Richmond Locomotive and Machine Works, 236
Richmond theater, 138
  burning of, 101
Richmond Times-Dispatch, 330
Richmond Whig, 11, 93, 108
Ritchie, Thomas, 11, 93
Rives, Amélie, 16, 256, 257
"Roadside Types" (sketch), 216, 217
Roane, Chief Justice Spencer, 11
Roanoke, 8, 15, 225, 330
Roanoke Island, 26, 29
Roanoke plantation, 101, 107
Roanoke River, damming of, 300, 301
Roanoke Valley, 224, 225
Robertson, John, 13
Robinson, Bill "Bojangles," 17, 322
Rochambeau, Comte de, 82–83
Rockbridge County, 12, 16, 71, 126, 231
Rockefeller, John D., Jr., 17, 308
Rockefeller, Nelson, 320
Rockefeller restoration (Williamsburg), 17, 307, 308, 309
"Rockfish Gap and the Mountain House" (illustration), 126–27
Rockingham County, 12, 102
Rocky Mount, 222
Rogers, William Barton, 110, 111
Rolfe, John, 3, 32, 239
Roma (dirigible), 290, 291
Romantic Revolution in America, The (Parrington), 6, 13
Roosevelt, Franklin D., 18, 302, 312, 313
Roosevelt, Mrs. Franklin D., 312, 313
Roosevelt, Theodore, 278
Rosewell mansion, 5, 252–53
Ruffin, Edmund, 13
Ruffner, Henry, 13
Ruffner, Reverend William Henry, 16, 231
Ruins (Richmond), 193, 194–95, 196, 197
Ryan, Abram Joseph, 296

S. Harris Cheap Store, 232, 233
Saarinen, Eero, 319
St. Charles Hotel, 208–9
St. John's Church (Henrico Parish Church), 72
St. Luke's Church (Newport Parish Church), 17, 38, 39
St. Paul's Church (London), 3
Salisbury, battle of, 8
Saloons, 276
Sandy, Sir Edwin, 36, 37
Saratoga, battle of, 78
"Scenes of the Occupation," 154, 155
Scheff, Fritzi, 296
Schell, T. B., 226
Science, 6, 274–75
Schirra, Walter, 319
Schofield, General John, 15
School buses, 284, 328–29

Schools. *See* Education
Schooners, 265
Scope Center (Norfolk), 325
Scotch-Irish immigrants, 4, 6, 7–8,
26, 61, 64, 91, 95, 110, 112,
138, 199
Scotland Street (Williamsburg), 5
Scott, George C., **322**
Scott, Sir Walter, 13
Scott, General Winfield, 13, 14
Scribner's Monthly, 225
See also Picture Credits
Sea battles
of ironclads, 14, 149, 155, 156–
57
Revolutionary War, 80–81
"Sea of China and the Indies, The"
(map of 1651), **28**, **29**
Secession Ordinance (1861), 13,
142, **143**
Second Continental Congress, 9
Second Market (Richmond), 276
Secretariat (thoroughbred), 320
Segregation, 16
Seibel, Fred, 330, **331**
Senate chamber (Richmond), 86
Serapis (ship), 10
Seven Pines, battle of, 14, **160**, **161**
Seventh Street (Richmond), 271,
272, **273**
Sevier, John, 12
Sevier family, 7
Shack, **300**, **301**
Shad, fishing for, **234**, **235**
Shakespeare, William, 3
Shark (thoroughbred), **53**
Sharp Top peak, 24–25
Shenandoah County, 102
Shenandoah National Park, 300,
302, **303**
Shenandoah River, 285
Shenandoah Valley, in Civil War,
178, **179**, 180–81
Shepard, Alan, 319
Sheppard, William Ludwell, 206,
211, 213, 217, 218
Sheridan, General Philip, 179, 180
Shipbuilding, 16, 124–25, 265, 288,
319
Shirley Highway, 314
Shirley plantation, 5, **52**, **53**
Shockoe Valley, 147
Short, William, 6
Sigel, General Franz, 165
Sinclair, John, 10
Sir Archy (horse), **254**, **255**
Sixth Street (Richmond), 275
Sixth Street Market, 276, **277**
Skyline Drive, 126
Slaves and slavery, 4, 9, 11, 12, 83,
116–19, 143, **197**
abolitionist movement, 12, 13,
117, 119, 141
electoral power of, 12
emancipation, 13, 16, 169, 183,
206, 218
en route to Tennessee, 117
fugitives, 56, **57**, 147
for harvesting wheat, 118, 119

importing of, 56
market, 117, 119
Missouri Compromise, 11–12
Nat Turner rebellion, 13, **116**,
117
North's trade in, 13
overseer, 116, 117
pen for, **119**
plantation life of, 118–19
quarters for, 117
recruitment into federal ranks,
168, **169**
writers' defense of, 13
Slayton, Donald, 319
Slemp, C. Bascom, **302**
Slipware pottery, 35
Smith, Adam, 6
Smith, Francis, 231
Smith, Governor George William,
101
Smith, John, 3, 31, **32**, **33**, 35
Smith, Reverend Samuel Stanhope,
64
Smith, Governor William H., 193
Smithfield plantation, 64, **65**, 245,
250, 281
Smythe, Sir Thomas, 30, 31, 37
Snead, Chief Justice Harold, 328
Snead, Sam, 322, **323**
Sousa, John Philip, 228, **229**
South Carolina, 3, 8, 13, 89, 143,
205, 296
South Pole, 3
South Richmond, 133
Southampton County, 13, 14, 117,
188
Southern Literary Messenger, 13
Southern Planter (magazine), **244**,
245
Southside Railroad Depot (Rich-
mond), 191
Spanish-American War, 270–71, 276
Spotswood, Governor Alexander, 3,
7, 8, 9, 18, 44, **45**, 56
Spotswood Hotel, 211
bill of fare, **234**, **235**
Springs, Elliott, 296, **297**
Stamp Act, 6, 9
Stranger, Russell, **325**
Stanley, Thomas B., **330**
State house. *See* Capitol building
Statute for Religious Freedom, 91
Staunton, 10, 17, 117, 126, 138,
287, 327
Steam engine, 162
Steamboats, 281
Stearns, Junius Brutus, 119
Stemming of tobacco, **239**, 243
Stern, General Jo Lane, 256, **257**
Stevenson, Andrew, **134**, **135**
Stewart, John, 199
Stover, Jacob, 7
Straight Cut No. 1 (cigarettes),
240, 241
Stratford Hall, **59**
Street cars, 272, **273**
Stuart, General James Ewell Brown
"Jeb," 14, 166, 174, **175**
statue of, 263

Stuttgart Ballet, **324**, **325**
Styron, William, 16
Suffolk, 129, 245
Suffrage, 15, 292–93
"Sun Do Move, The" (sermon), 222
Supper room (Governor's Palace),
46, **47**
Surry, 4
Surry County, 39
Surveying, 67
Susan Constant (ship), 3
Sussex County, 249
Swan Tavern, 276
Swanson, Mrs. Claude, 310
Swimming, 280, **281**, 300
Swinging bridges, 266–67
Sword (Civil War), 152, **153**
Sydnor and Hundley (furniture
store), 273
Syms-Eaton Free School, **110**

Tamanend (Indian), **125**
Tangier Island, 337
Tarleton, Colonel Banastre, 10, 53,
78
Tatham, William, 97
Taverns, 60–61, 64, **65**, 75, 104
Taylor, John, 6
Taylor, Zachary, 9
Tazewell County, 333
Teach, Edward. *See* Blackbeard
Technology, 272–73
Telephone switchboard, **272**
Tempest, The (Shakespeare), 3
Temple, Shirley, **322**
Tennessee, 3, 8, 12, 14, 117, 225
Tennis, 322
Tenth Street (Richmond), 276
Terrapin, 235
Texas, 3, 12
Textile industry, 332–33
Thacher, Oxenbridge, 9
Thackeray, William Makepeace, 133,
135
Thetis Bay (ship), 68–69
Thomas, General George H., 14
Thoroughgood, Adam, 39
Thoroughgood house, 38–39
Thumb Run, 267
Tide mill, 267
Tilghman, Tench, 82–83
Timetable, railroad, **236**, **237**
Tintypes, 268
Tobacco, 6, 12, 96–97, 120, 238–43,
300
cigarette manufacturing, 242–43
drying and storing houses, 96,
97
factories, 239, 332, **333**
growth and curing, 238–39, 334
importing slaves to work, 56
introduction of, 32
luxury from (eighteenth century),
52–55
map of farms and plantations
(1681), **40**
marketing, 239, 240, 241, 334
shipping, 5, 56, 69, 97

Tobacco (*Continued*)
warehouse receipts, 56, 57
wealth from, 4, 40–41, 56–57, 243
Tobacco Exchange (Richmond), 240
Tobacconists labels (seventeenth and eighteenth centuries), **40, 41, 56**
Tom Jones (Fielding), 4, 55
Tower Hill plantation, 248–49
"Trail of the Lonesome Pine, The" (song), 296
Transportation Command (U.S. Army), 288
Traveller (horse), **164, 165**
Treaty of 1677, 37
Tredegar Iron Works, 132, 133, 152, **153, 177**
Trolleys, electric, 272, **273**
Troubadours (Washington and Lee University), **258–59**
Troubetzkoy, Amélie Rives, 16, **256, 257**
Troubetzkoy, Prince Pierre, 257
Truck farming, 334, **335**
Tuck, Governor William M., 324, **325, 330**
Tuckahoe mansion, **250–51**
Tucker, Henry St. George, 298, **299**
Tucker, John Randolph, 298, **299**
Tucker, Nathaniel Beverley, 13, 110, **111**
Tucker, St. George, 6, 110
Tucker family, 250
Tudor architecture, 39
Turcotte, Ron, **320**
Turner, Nat, 13, 117
Turner's Rebellion 13, **116, 117**
Tweedy, Mrs. Penny Chenery, **320**
Tyler, John, 3, 9, 10, 13, 129, **134, 135**, 231
at Virginia Constitutional Convention (1828–30), **106–7**
Tyler, Lyon Gardiner, 231, 260, **261, 305**

Underground Railway, 119
Underwood, John C., 15
Underwoood, Oscar, 298, **299**
Underwood Constitution, 15, 16, 202
United States (liner), 333
U.S. Army Air Corps, 290
U.S. Arsenal (Harper's Ferry), **140, 141, 148**
burning of, 149
U.S. Congress, 3, 15, 17, 93, 98, 135, 141, 173, 293, 302
U.S. Constitution, 10, 11, 98
U.S. Customs House and Treasury Building (Richmond), **133**
U.S. Debarkation Hospital (Hampton), 288, **289**
U.S. Highway 1, 285
U.S. House of Representatives, 93, 135, 302
U.S. Marine Band, 228, **229**
U.S. Marines, **140, 141**
U.S. Naval Academy, 125
U.S. Navy, 125, 310, 319

U.S. Senate, 17
U.S. Supreme Court, 11, 15, 16, 17
University Center of Virginia, 327
University College of Medicine, 275
University of Richmond, 12, 295
University of Virginia, 110, **112,** 287, 295
Jefferson's design for, **91**
Unknown Soldier, Tomb of, **338, 339**
Urban corridor, 17, 316–17, 333

Valentine, Edward Virginius, 205, **275**
Valentine Museum, 275
Valley camapign. *See* Peninsula campaign
Valley of Virginia, 7, 8, 14, 21, 64, 102, 110, 126, 320
farm at spring plowing time, 21, **22–23**
hills in, **24–25**
Van Lew, Elizabeth, 174
Van Meter, John and Isaac, 7
Vaterland (ship), 302, **303**
Victory Monument (Yorktown), **228**
Vincennes, Ind., 9
Virginia, naming of, 3, 29, 31
Virginia (DeBry), **26**
Virginia (ironclad), 14, 149, 155, **156–57**
Virginia Arsenal, **197**
Virginia Assembly, 5, 9, 10, 11, 12, 13, 293, 313
authorized, 37
chambers at Williamsburg, 46, **48, 49**
first meeting of, 4, 36, 37, 39
Virginia Beach, 280, **281**
Virginia Boat Club, **281**
Virginia Capes, battle of (1781), 10, **80–81**
map of, 80, **81**
Virginia Company, 3, 4, 31
Virginia Constitutional Convention of 1828–30, 12, **106–7**
Virginia Constitutional Convention of 1867–68 (Underwood Convention), 15, 202, **203**
Virginia Convention of 1775, 9, **72**
Virginia Convention of 1776, 6, 9, **75**
Virginia Convention of 1788, 10
Virginia Gazette, 64
advertisements in, 53, 56, 57, 71
announcement of mental hospital, **70, 71**
patriot version of, **72**
Virginia Historical Society, 304, **305**
Virginia Hospital, 275
Virginia Manufactory of Arms, 133
Virginia Military Institute (VMI), 12, 112, **113,** 179, 263, **294,** 295
class of 1901, **286, 287**
leaders, **231**
Virginia Museum, 325
Virginia Polytechnic Institute and State University, 230, **231**

regimental band, **326, 327**
Virginia Street (Richmond), 240
Virginia Supreme Court, 11
Virginians, The (Thackeray), **135**
Vocational training, 215
Voter registration, 206, **207, 222**

Wakefield, 67
Walker, Gilbert C., 214, **215**
Walker, Maggie Mitchell, **231**
Walker, Dr. Thomas, 3, 60, **61,** 63
Walker Creek, **266–67**
Wallace, "Bigfoot," 3
Wallops Island Launch Facility, **319**
War of 1812, 98–99, 104
Warehouses, tobacco, 240, **241**
receipts from, 56, 57
Warm Springs, 128, **129,** 296
bath house at, **71**
Warrenton, 218
Warrenton Gold Cup race, **320**
Warrior's Path (Indian trail), 7, 8
Washington, Betty, 53
Washington, Booker T., 17, **222**
Washington, George, 6, 10, 11, 17, 18, 53, 55, 91, 93, 95, 104, 112, 120, 147, 255
background of, **66–67**
birthplace, 66, **67,** 89
as commander in chief, 9, 67, 77, **82–83, 84–85,** 89
death of, 89
field desk, **67**
in French and Indian Wars, 8, **66,** 67
home of, 17, **68–69,** 88, 89, 95, **118, 119,** 327
land holdings, 88, 89
may by, 67
sculpture of, **338**
Washington, Lawrence, 89
Washington, Martha, 89
Washington, Mary Ball, 95
Washington, D.C., 11, 12, 13, 14, 143, 144, 162, 171, 180, 202, 205, 228, 268, 275, 314, 317, 318
British capture of, 98, **99**
early view of, **92–93**
fear of Confederate attack, **182–83**
map of, 92, **93**
Washington house (Fredericksburg), **95**
Washington and Lee University, 12, 112, **113,** 259, **294,** 295
Chapel, **205**
Lee as president of, 165, 204, **205**
Washington Monument, **24**
Water sports, **280–81, 300**
Waterford, early buildings in, **60, 61**
Watermills, **267**
Wattle-and-daub chimneys, **268**
Waud, Alfred R., 201, **202**
Weldon, N.C., 15
West Franklin Street (Richmond), **296**
West Point, Va., **171**

West Point Military Academy, 147, 158, 199
West Virginia, xii, 63, 129
  secession of, 14, 172, 173, 202
West Washington Street (Petersburg), 190–91
Westmoreland Club, 275
Westmoreland County, 4, 6, 59, 67, 89, 104
Westover plantation, 59, 250
Wetherburn's Tavern, 259
Weyer's Cave, 126, 127
Whaley, Matthew, 231
Wheat harvesting, 118, 119
Wheeling Convention of 1861, 14, 172, 173, 202
Wheeling Convention of 1862, 15
Whig party, 93
White, John, 26
White House, Va., 171
White Sulphur Springs, 128, 129, 205, 322
  tea party at, 256, 257
White Top Music Festival, 300
Whiting, Thomas, 10
Whitney, Eli, 245
Wickham, General Williams Carter, 236
Wickham railroad depot, 236, 237
Widows (Civil War), 197
Wig-making, 338
Wilderness Road, 8, 61, 63, 226–27
  Union capture of, 173
Willcox Landing, 185
William III, King, 4, 5
William and Mary, College of, 6, 42, 46, 50, 98, 110, 111, 217, 261, 305

faculty, 231
fire of 1705, 51
first professor of medicine, 70, 71
first structure, 44
founded, 4
graduation program, 114
President Coolidge at, 295
women admitted to, 294, 295
Wren Building, 232, 308, 309
William and Mary Quarterly, 305
Williams, Camilla, 17
Williamsburg, 5, 6, 7, 9, 11, 37, 42, 44–51, 53, 56, 69, 72, 76, 104, 108, 110, 173, 217, 231, 250, 261, 313, 338
colonial life in, 50–51
in late 1800s, 232–33
map of Middle Plantation site, 44
mental hospital, 70, 71, 232, 233
naming of, 5
as new capital, 5, 46–49
principal buildings about 1744, 44–45
public gaol, 51
restoration, 17, 307, 308, 309
St. George Tucker House, ii
Williamsburg theater, 51
Wilson, Woodrow, 9, 17, 138, 287
birthplace, 287
Wilson Foundation, 287
Wilton house, 5
Winchester, 8, 78, 130, 296, 299, 334
Civil War battles at, 166, 180
Wisconsin, 9
Wise, Governor Henry, 136, 140, 141, 204, 205
Wise County, 302, 322

Wolf Trap Farm Park for the Performing Arts, 325
Wolfe, Tom, 16
Woodstock, 8, 78
Wool, General John, 151
World War I, 232, 257, 284, 288–89, 302, 338
World War II, 16, 281, 310–11, 313, 333
embarkation of troops, 310, 311
trainees, 310
World's Fair, 228, 255
"Wreck of Old 97, The" (folk song), 290
Wren Building (College of William and Mary), 232, 308, 309
Wright brothers, 288
Wythe, George, 6, 10, 13
Wythe County, 225
Wytheville, 224, 225

Yeardley, Governor Sir George, 3, 37
York County, 59
York River, 4, 5, 44, 56, 162, 253
tobacco trade on, 40
Yorktown-Gloucester bridge over, 314
Yorktown, 5, 11, 158
bridge between Gloucester and, 314
centennial, 228–29
federal fortification of, 158, 159
pre-Revolutionary port at, 56–57
siege victims, 306, 307
surrender at, 10, 17, 80, 82–83, 84–85, 104, 105, 228, 307
Yorktown (ironclad), 155
Yorktown Theater, 228, 229